A SUPERINTENDENT'S EYES

steve dalachinsky

UNBEARABLE BOOKS / AUTONOMEDIA
Series Editors: Jim Feast and Ron Kolm

UB – 1: *Spermatagonia: The Isle of Man,* bart plantenga
UB – 2: *Negativeland,* Doug Nufer
UB – 3: *Neo Phobe,* Jim Feast and Ron Kolm
UB – 4: *Shorts Are Wrong,* Mike Topp
UB – 5: *The Hotel of Irrevocable Acts,* Carl Watson
UB – 6: *The Ass's Tale,* John Farris
UB – 7: *This Young Girl Passing,* Donald Breckenridge
UB – 8: *Love Does Not Make Me Gentle or Kind,* Chavisa Woods
UB – 9: *A Superintendent's Eyes,* Steve Dalachinsky

Forthcoming
UB — 10: *Kali's Day,* Bonny Finberg

A SUPERINTENDENT'S EYES

steve dalachinsky

(revised & expanded)

photographs by arthur kaye

Unbearable Books / Autonomedia

ISBN: 978-1-57027-253-0
Second Edition published 2013 Autonomedia / Unbearable Books

All Photographs: Arthur Kaye
Cover Design: Jim Fleming

NYSCA
New York State Council on the Arts

This publication is made possible in part with public funds from the New York State Council on the Arts, a state agency.

Unbearables
www.unbearables.com

Autonomedia
POB 568 Williamsburgh Station
Brooklyn, NY 11211-0568 USA

info@autonomedia.org
www.autonomedia.org

192

The author would like to thank Hozomeen Press & Rich Martin for publication of the first edition of this book in 2000, & Ron Kolm (a super himself), Jim Feast & Jim Fleming for this republication with additions & edits, some 13 years later.

Special thanks to my wife Yuko Otomo who endured most of this with me & who at times helped shovel snow & haul out the garbage.

Contents

Steve,

Personally, you're a great guy... as a Super you suck. Abraham and you have got to work this Super thing out. I'm paying $2K a month for shit. For the fifth time in less than two weeks, there was no hot water this morning. When one's paying $2K a month rent, one fucking expects hot water in the morning. I shower at 7AM... whether you sleep until 11AM or not. Call me crazy...I don't like working all day long without a morning shower. I know you don't give a damn, but take pity on your neighbors and at least clarify your non-arrangement with Abraham. The friggin' hallways are disgusting and haven't been swept... maybe ever? You know, Steve, if you don't want the job at least resolve! Good God man... this doesn't require magic... setting the hot water regulator to deliver hot water 24 hours a day ain't rocket science... I bet Frankie could even figure this one out. Is my only/best recourse to write Abraham? Feel free to call me and rant back....

Andrew

(abraham is the landlord.
frankie his ex-con, crackhead handyman.)

A Superintendent's Eyes

notes, letters, rants, poems, observations & other laborious detailings
of a dissatisfied servant of the people......

i live in one of the richest neighborhoods in n.y. because i can't afford to live anywhere
else

I AM NOT WHAT I DO

"many different storylines unfold in many different ways....."

I don't analyze you so don't analyze Me

"When sticking your foot in your mouth always make room for the other." — D.G.

that 5th floor window filled only with moonlight

i just work here

Dog Death Chimera Corner of the Eye
inescapable goal grasped

materiality of *words* written (the *written word*)

a superintendent's eyes # ? *sidewalk* ⟶
decided to occupy the sidewalk for awhile

A SUPERINTENDENT'S EYES #1
(from the basement of the academy)

1.

at the corner
                    from the corner of my eyes
                                        a crowd passes

2.

you fine poets who live among universities
you glorious academicians
can you see civilization in your own backyards
in the ethnic eyes of the shopkeeper
buried in one neighborhood forever
dryly breathing
under a petrified cross?

the years have changed
but the times have not.

1

A SUPERINTENDENT'S EYES #2
(my cell door)

the tenant in #11 knocks on my door wearing ugly pants & ugly shoes. he looks real stoned & says he wants to cop 2 z's but the people haven't called him back yet so he thinks he'll have to postpone it for another day. he looks really "hip" & lost. i say fine anytime & don't forget to bring back my Stones album when you're done with it.

his super kitsch zoot suit pants are a seedy subdued black & white stripe tapered @ the bottom & his white canvas shoes are tapered @ the toe. wingtips gone bad. styles dredged up from another era. lost on the body of his stone blue eyes. trapped in the "club" syndrome until the next fad pops up. his anxious small town coolness trying so hard to be new york. he lives with a pale-skinned uptight failed opera singing diva & his love of guns & hatred of anything not "white" lurk behind his eyes like a tear-soaked death aria. he's a pop culture puppy trying hard to catch a milk bone.

as he turns to leave he says "oh by the way my faucet's been leaking for about a week now. do you think you could come up & look @ it when you get a chance?"

"SURE."

A SUPERINTENDENT'S EYES #3
(a basket of pomegranates)

1.

the world outside
a basket of pomegranates
flung beneath the wheels of trucks
mingling with the heads of winos this calm spring day

the pigeons return
circling the roof
home again.

2.

white
the place where resting turned green & o pen
today
among the streets

a pleasure

3.

6 or 7 a.m. a knock awakens me i rise rubbing my
bleary eyes open the door
— *you'd better get out there & clean the sidewalk*
before the building gets a ticket —
huh — *go out & look* — i get dressed — head out

a shambles of dark green plastic, food & all manner of
garbage fills the street
in front of the building like the first tattered
shadows cast on a mild spring day
once again the bags have been slashed to pieces
by those seeking treasure

A SUPERINTENDENT'S EYES #4
(after the flood)

i walked into your room drenched from the rain you smiled timidly

i offered you my hand but you wanted my heart

you offered me your soul but i wanted your body

we offered our breaths but wanted our lives

we helpless people cut from the same ***MOLD***

we offer only what we have but it is never enough

we must move on

ruptured by promises & dreams we are left with only our selves to face

i give you cherries but you want the tree

we are conceived in spirit born in flesh then disappear

she confronts her canvas paints the blue parts black

i check for damage that the storm may have caused

A SUPERINTENDENT'S EYES #5
(a series of accidents)

she throws away the trash   among it is my new haiku

i break my favorite coffee mug

the spider crawls along my finger

the cassette tape gets mangled

the window chain snaps

monk breaks down notes while breaking down melodies

my good friend breaks up with his wife

the speaker falls off the shelf & smashes my typewriter

2 ships melting on the water

A SUPERINTENDENT'S EYES #6
(it used to be that way)

1. vinyl

2 ex-junkies get together
smoke fills the room
ashes fall to the floor

the jewish junkie with the tattoos has been clean for 5 days
after a 360 day jones
he's just shaved off his beard
& thinks he'll have it together in another 360

he's real sweet & loves his 3 snakes & his parrot

his only complaint is that his ex old lady won't give him back
his record collection
his stereo
& his '55 mercury
what bugs him most are the lps

the other ex-junkie understands perfectly well
as he tries to sell him some of his.

2. Methadone Bobby Did It

the pupils try to hide within his eyes

2 black dots that follow themselves around
like awkward endless circles
the food comes up
the sun comes out
sun
up food out
garbage men begin scraping messages along the sidewalk
i walk in circles awkwardly the endless night has ended again
the sun comes up the food comes out
food up sun out pupils cry to hide inside the eyes
(thank g*d for liquids)
2 black dots follow themselves around start & stop **2 black ..s**

A SUPERINTENDENT'S EYES #7
(in hot water again)

the hot water is off again
as always #11 calls to let me know

i enter the boiler room
push the red button
& the hell fires flare up

rubbing my hands together
i quickly exit the basement
anticipating the wintry
night.

A SUPERINTENDENT'S EYES #8
(steve's blues)

1.

god light holy buttons used to open & close the soul
wife neon molecule sign not for white men only

i stand divorced from myself notquitewhite
against the phantoms
dancing & fidgeting with my buttons
day fall into night & i sing:

"pussy cat's copulatin' wid da cockroach
steel band playin in da clothes closet
admission is the price of one head
& the entrance is thru the ashtray....."

2.

like a cigarette commercial
i stand by the sea watching men fish
& waves break high against the rocks

the dog follows the frisbee
until it loses itself in the tide

face washed by warm night wind
feet digging into wet sand
i gag on smoking fear & dream of things i never had
& maybe never will
while warm spiked thoughts intercept my station break
& return me to the program in progress.

A SUPERINTENDENT'S EYES #9
(smoke gets in your lungs or old habits die hard)

1. jackie,

i'm sitting here 2:45 a.m. listening to Muddy Waters looking at the dead white snow pile up in front of the house knowing that in the morning it will be my task to clear it i'm writing in the dark thinking as usual about life death youth & you the table warbles your poems of compassion which at first i did not understand or appreciate now cause my heart to warble petty thief in winter alone too cold your poems too heady for me my mojo not working i drink grapefruit juice & smoke another cigarette a long chain of smoke fills my lungs & then the air it's nice to be with someone & sad yet nice to be alone the cats have gone off into the bedroom another chain of events i suppose we eventually all go somewhere if we are not yet there i barely understand anything even *DICK & JANE* which is the essence of life alludes me there's one cigarette in my mouth & one behind my ear this is not a detective novel though everything seems like a mystery i watch lots of movies mostly on tv listen a lot to JAZZ read very little never write or write too much no job though i guess mopping up after others counts for something & i remember you once telling me that you & the father of your first kid lived in the Village & that he had a beard was very smart wrote a lot or not enough & was also a superintendent i think i even may have met him once — too bad our kid was a miscarriage you 19 sitting there on the toilet both of us watching its little life slip out of you — well we've since

managed to survive despite all we've been through strange
this survival thing this ongoing routine does anyone ever
have enough.....muddy waters

good night   or   good morning as some folks would say.

2. the undead

5 days without a cigarette
listening to **Ten Years After**
1st attempt at writing without smoking
somehow feel poetry & cigarettes are inextricable
not quite sure if they are the same thing
or if one accompanies the other

listening to the lp ***UNDEAD***
feel   stiff   absence of smoke & burning eyes

no thoughts come
cigarettes & inspiration 1 & the same?
cigarette ***muse***

time & 40 cigarettes a day
little sleep
& constant harassment by tenants
the moon rising swift & slow
behind the black sharp edges of the
blding
worsening cough
yellow stained fingers
wild leaf tamed
burgeoning ashtray

is this how poems are sprung?

A SUPERINTENDENT'S EYES #10
(the old man in the hall)

small browned old man with broken teeth
white stubble porcupines from chin
frightened face
fragile soft grey/green eyes
tired wet too much LIFE

tight loose veins on crooked hands
matted grey hair beneath crumpled grey hat
soiled beige shirt
blue grey suit
with a bright gold button in his lapel
stating in bold black letters

MI DIOS ES REAL

sorry you'll have to leave i tell him.

A SUPERINTENDENT'S EYES #11
(the key)

will someone
EVER   fix
my mailbox
(any help would
be appreciated) — apt. #2

his mailbox lock
has been broken for months

his patience
like his overflowing mail
has been,
thankfully,
boundless.

A SUPERINTENDENT'S EYES #12
(the eve of st. anthony's feast*)

that time so long ago
when you saved my life
is no longer important

the stalls along the empty street
make this place feel like a ghost
town

the clouds sitting here in my eyes
cover the entire city

my old lady talks japanese to the tv

men who have nothing
find something in anything
at the risk of still wanting too much

this nigger ripped the shirt off johnny lines' back

johnny lines says his old lady jerks off to Johnny Carson
paying homage to his-snatch-a-dollah-holiness

all you wanderers returning home from exile ***WAKE UP!***

tomorrow is as good as ever

*this feast due to politics both mob-related & governmental no longer exists

A SUPERINTENDENT'S EYES #13
(the gamble)

a. ***WAKE UP*** *you armchair commanders!*

to love somebody or rock & roll equally as well as
da vinci or dracula alike & speak of blake &
pussy
in the same breath & quaaludes & diamonds
chew diamonds & call a club a heart

sirens   damn sirens   going off all night

& the smoke from a dirty boiler

things slowly becoming rapid & closing

light & time fading to obscurity

i sleep with the breath of seasons upon my face

or rather   dream of sleeping

retiring to some other
place
& left behind
a prison   or

window
perhaps

a tiny hole in the screen
for the Plague
to wander thru
& drain some of my
blood

b. the dead cat

the avocado growing on the window sill will never make it.
the cat ate its leaves & died.
she's no 3rd ave. whore......
could never be.

c. the new girls in #13

i am elegiac in my pent-up meetings with people
but
this dish really came on tactful & not too heavy so
i unstressed myself by digging
her self
& her roommates' arses

(iamb elegiac pentameter distich dactyl arsis)

they (she) leave(s) me this note:

Just to give you advanced notice we (apt#13) are having a party tonight. We will try to keep the noise level as low as possible and we will turn the music off before it gets very late.

Apt # 13

there's a blizzard outside
all day long i am telling myself
be kind
be polite.........i knock on their door & thank them for the note

A SUPERINTENDENT'S EYES #14
(2nd ave. deli* — the blizzard continues...)

do those touched by madness
recognize others likewise touched?

the woman sitting with me
in the deli
keeps saying   whew it's a real BLIZZARD
i turn absently toward the street
& go   um   hum   umhum

my   headache worsens
my neck equally tightens
the old old waiter
climbs inside of me
as i keep saying Thank YOU.

*the owner of the 2nd ave. deli was murdered his killer was never found. a bank has replaced it. the deli ironically has moved to e. 33rd st. & 3rd ave.

A SUPERINTENDENT'S EYES #15
(shoveling snow)

snatches of conversation
overheard while
shoveling snow

"......they never wear coats...my chauffeur last night

he didn't wear one."

"Yes I'm going skydiving next week," he says

she "I was going to but I changed my mind. Would you
like to know why?"

"Well it might not be a Rothschild but it has
the appearance of one."

i comment to a passerby after shoveling
for the 4th time today:
it's like that poem about how useless the rain is
as it falls into the ocean
he remarks "well we're lucky it still happens.
imagine a world without it."

even in a blizzard money seems to disappear
dogs' noses disappear

one red glove in a snowdrift

A SUPERINTENDENT'S EYES #16
(a digression)

the poet's eyes
are all chipped & stained
glass

2 stars burning
2 cat's eye marbles
a grecian urn
a greasy tablecloth in a cheap cafe

the wheels of time
turning eternally
from childhood to old age
birth to death

the poet's eyes are
wet & whispering tongues of 2 great bells

burnt out bulbs

broom handles

my eyes watch the veins in a slice of pizza
melt
before dropping down
& rolling away……..

A SUPERINTENDENT'S EYES #17
(the best policy)

i told mark that i was somewhat dishonest

he said   that's o.k. everyone is a little   i guess.......

A SUPERINTENDENT'S EYES #18
(a note to the tenants)

whatever kind christian soul scattered
their christmas tree remains
all over the hall has no concern for either
christmas christ or me
& has no business having a christmas tree
in the first place.
try a plastic one next time.

remember: a season for caring
a season for sharing

*thanks to those who tipped me & please remember the mailman.**

in red ink someone scrawls:

YOU MEAN THE ALCOHOLIC WHO'S ALWAYS LATE...

* louis, the mailman who also served in the reserves finally retired.

A SUPERINTENDENT'S EYES #19
(in the wilderness)

left alone in the wilderness
        wilderness being a neighborhood
        a new neighbor jars me with a neighborly hello

        alone in the wilderness
        wilderness being
        the dust & concrete floor
        of the boiler room
        humble almost invisible
            the dead mouse

A SUPERINTENDENT'S EYES #20
(crazy cat)

my name's crazy cat
i'm from da south bronx
i blongd to a club
i was arrested 31x for assault
sure i did time
28 months of a 4 year stretch
for stabbin a dude
the club is my family
the ghetto brothers took me in
when i was a kid
den i switch to da nomads
& den help start da savage skulls
i was war counselor
i ha' respect
i din't quit
i retired
why 'cause i'm married now &
i love my wife
i got a job
counslin' kids
on rivinton & pitt
i do art wid dem
i teach 'em how to do art
on t-shirts
da right way
i have a tatoo of hearts & roses
on my forearm
surroundin a swastika

recently
my brother passed away
stabbed on
halloween
killed &
passed
away

A SUPERINTENDENT'S EYES #21
(rotgut & sleaze)

America is the driest source of art in all of history.

writing is tiring....thinking is much easier.

did Pollock really push painting to its boundaries?

for decades now the Europeans have been looking toward "US"
for artistic inspiration why? we have nothing better
than Michelangelo
to offer them....talking is much easier....they all want to be
like Chernowski
while maintaining their old world intellectual facade....Jack who?
oh, is that guy still around?

we're all so desperately sad...
what's so special about puking anyway....?

thinking & talking are much easier....but they can never
make you immortal.

talent

the big time
chairs die a lot

a diet of what is
& what should be
encompassing
what wasn't

light hangs low
& blinks
backward

fame
10% talent
90% luck

100% connections

sometimes one has sometimes one is

A SUPERINTENDENT'S EYES #22
(caged)

i feel like a caged beast having to sit around the apt. all day waiting for a delivery or a repairman....pacing the kitchen or the hallway…standing out front on the steps lips pursed tightly mumbling into my throat...i bang my head against transparent walls like a caged beast....growling where are you where are you no meat thrown my way.....missing a step groin bulging...caged beast inside this overpriced zoo… small puff of life still so immersed in bodily functions & "religion"...heart-seam splitting...masked like sad yugen amongst crowded verse...sound/color feeling without hearing...let me out i need to get a s(p)lice...i need to go to the post office.......the girl with the flowers i need her....see me see me see me...

i can see the caged beast in raindrops
on the old bridge
behind the tree
in a faraway
place

hot   cold   yawning   i start & stop   like the rain
am soft & hard like the sky

caged beast   a caged beast   so hungry & so ill at ease....

A SUPERINTENDENT'S EYES #23
(the near-suicide in apt. 19)

another one of those silly people
who'd rather live without trees
than with them.

the old chinese man collects ginkgo berries
in front of the park
across the street.

the drunk with the bottle of **irish rose**
& face like a bowl of bruised fruit
sits against the wall
beneath the crabapple tree
he points at the tree
& says smiling
"that's my tree"

A SUPERINTENDENT'S EYES #24
(jesus dream — they know not what they do)

i had a hard time waking up. this is nothing new. i have a hard time waking up every morning. today is another " miracle" day. sometimes i enjoy these days depending on the response i receive from the crowd. sometimes i detest them because of all the preparation & trickery involved. like the timing & precision involved in walking on water. or the loaf of bread routine if i'm not wearing a tunic with wide enough sleeves. water conditions also play a role. like calm water's better than wavy. & suppose the Boss wakes up hung over & decides to switch the itinerary on me at the last minute. say the hooker shows up instead of the blind man. or maybe the leper doesn't have enough spots.

& all those interviews & dealings with unsavory characters.

& today the hardest stunt of all....hanging around all day in the hot sun without anything to eat or drink...getting my heart pierced for the umpteenth time then waiting for someone to come up the hill pull out the nails & carry me off to the cave.

ah the cave. what a relief to be in that cave. no more thorns...just laying around for 3 days until it's time to perform the neatest trick of all......

A SUPERINTENDENT'S EYES #25
(the night air)

on delancey st.
the hooker asks her
if she wants to join
an orgy
she replies
"my hands are full"
then turns to me
& says
"in this pitiful heaven
the sparrows
eat dirt"

A SUPERINTENDENT'S EYES #26
(my daily walk)

the shadow
thru the dirt-covered screen
is a man
walking like a shadow
thru a dirt-covered screen

how much space is left
in this document
this tv
digital groan

today is cold
grey
the sky is grey
the clouds dissolve
like a 20,000 yr. old
jawbone

i am a cloud
a jawbone

the shadow
becomes a pool
of dirty dots
the signature appears
on the
document

the promise
dissolves
on the stairwells

the stairwells need cleaning
again.

A SUPERINTENDENT'S EYES #27
(rm. #318 — his job)

in rm. #318
of the N.Y. Public Library
there's an exhibit called
50 Years of American Poetry
it is a bit exclusive

the room is closed off & cool
with great wood & glass showcases

there are letters & poems
typed & handwritten

there are books

all under glass

alone
in rm. #318
an old man in a blue uniform
dusts the nameplates
beneath the portraits
that surround
him.

A SUPERINTENDENT'S EYES #28
(more questions than answers)

1. housekeeping

men & women. they love to play house. i lived with
my first "woman" when i was 18. by 19 i staggered
off to california
  broken heart broken
  spirit broken HOME....

there's always at least one couple in the supermarket
not too bad looking that seems to be in LOVE.
i'm staring at one right now. in the pasta aisle.

my wife & i sometimes look that way when we're
wandering around the hardware store
together.

2. i can't

when my aunt yetta died she was already a memory. when my cat died i went into shock & couldn't even go to the vet to pick up his body. it was summer & really hot. my aunt is still a memory & a fond childhood one at that. she used to stand in the kitchen cracking her knuckles & watching soap operas while cooking. she was very small & so was i so she seemed very big. she really loved me. i hadn't seen her for a long time but called her every now & again. the last thing she said to

me was that she wanted to live long enough to attend her grandson's bar mitzvah. she did & died almost immediately after. i got to go to her funeral. it was a funeral of memories. afterward at her husband's house (a locksmith & son of a jewish mobster who was poisoned by the mob) one of my cousins, the ex-prize fighter who threw a fight & was paid off by the mob by being given a carwash, called me into a bedroom & asked me to roll up my sleeves. "what for?" i asked. **"TRACKS,"** he answered.
that same afternoon her youngest brother & my favorite uncle on my father's side, while staring out the window from my aunt's kitchen table pointed to the big trees outside. "see those trees" he said — "yeh" long haired druggy me replied "they're beautiful" — "well they look beautiful on the surface but underneath the ground they're fighting for space — their roots are strangling each other." i rose & went to get another bagel. to think this was the same guy who told me when i was about 15 & fresh out of the nut-house, after a game of hoops with some ghetto kids he worked with, that no matter how bad i felt i should never stay inside but that i should at least take a walk around the block every day. he said his mother, a great woman, had let him stay in his room for months as a kid & that it was detrimental. oddly he was the only person in the family to complete college. after that day he disowned the family & i never saw him again.
well since then i've taken those walks & though i love trees almost more than anything else in the world i always think about their roots.

i had seen my cat the day before he died. panting in the closet. all done in. skinny & very very quiet. eyes pleading. the next day he was dead. his heart they said. he had no claws, no balls & was very good at fetching. i hope they gave him a funeral.

my aunt had cancer.

tracks roots   veins   death   all means of conveyance
you can bury the body but you can't always bury the memories
further still the rain seeps into my so(u)les

3. near & far

it may have lain there for seconds. maybe moments.
surely not more.
as i bent to pick it up something at the base
of my spine cracked.
my left hand reached toward the ground
& my right toward my back.
i realized then that NOTHING was too near or too far.

2 men 1 young 1 old passed each other by.

4. string quartet

my life is so small. i don't think i could dance on it.
like a dime i'm not sure if i could stop on it.
it moves slowly in a lane meant for speed.
i crave it yet pull away from it.
i play it.
play it down.
play it all at once.

my life rests on the edge of 4 small chairs
in a little room.
sometimes it is dissonant

atonal
like a headache
unraveling.
sometimes dank, foreboding.
sometimes unbearably
sweet.

on the dark wet street   a flock of pigeons   start   then scatter

5. door frame

it is a green door on a green door frame
i walk toward it   ice forms on my
upper lip   i do not want to see dead things on the street
so i turn away   i'm traveling northwest
it's what's behind the blood that helps keep a person warm.

6. the bank line

what will you look like when time ticks more of your face
away? will your chin drop? your hair fall out? your armpits
still sweat? will you stop dressing & acting like a chic rene-
gade? what will you do when your knees sag & your leather
cracks? will there still be room for miracles? ideals? ideas?
will there be life after life? will there be music, wine, clubs,
walkers, bedpans, hearing aids, nurses' aides? will your lips
move? voice ring? your mouth. what about your mouth?
your endless lists? will you be able to change a lightbulb?
after standing in line for 25 minutes waiting to cash a check
i realized that my teller did not grasp the concept
of foreign money.

A SUPERINTENDENT'S EYES #29
(the shower stall)

i dreamt the shower stall they put me in. noose around
my neck & feet. suspended tightly top to toe.   my arms
spread clockwise set an alarm clock they had made of me.
all wound up i watched them as they ate themselves to sleep.
i myself dozed off until going off at 9 a.m. the time that they
had set me for. & i rang out with a merciless ring to let them
know of morning come. but wake they never did.

i dreamt you inside me & set me free me ticking away &
then we lay & dreamt.

A SUPERINTENDENT'S EYES #30
(lester)

lester was a jazz musician. he hung around the candy store a lot & was always out of work. he played stand up bass, flute & tenor. he dug pettiford, parter, richard davis, charles lloyd & 'trane. But the cat he personally knew & idolized was sonny rollins.

lester knew i loved jazz & would drop by my place to speak on it. one day he asked if he could use the phone, i said sure, if it's not long distance, he said no just calling brooklyn to speak to sonny....sonny i mused you mean   yes he said newk himself. i found this hard to believe but went along with it anyway. he dialed waited & when the phone was picked up on the other end started talking. suddenly he said wait sonny i have a friend here who'd like to say hello. i grabbed the phone in disbelief & said HELLO & a rich deep voice answered HI. i recognized it immediately & stammered about what an honor it was to talk to him. we spoke a couple of minutes & i returned the phone to lester who said something quick & then ended by saying O.K. sonny i'll speak to you soon.

lester was 22, white, bright, jewish, short, good looking, & a dope fiend a real heavy dope fiend. he was a nice guy but a bit of a weasel & always had a hard time making & keeping friends. when he wasn't busy getting high or making or talking music he was busy hassling or hustling people. he & i got close for awhile. after my old lady split lester'd come over my apt. & we'd put on dolphy or something & get really fucked up on goofballs & junk. sometimes he'd even crash at my place.

once while my ex dropped by (she'd heard i was getting high & was worried), lester came around the same time. he had with him a quantity of lps that he wanted to sell because he needed the cash. they were mostly sonny rollins originals from his personal collection. i looked them over then asked are you sure you wanna part with these this is your life man — he smiled a timid smile said he needed the bread & that he couldn't think of anyone he'd rather see have them. i gave him a reasonable sum & he thanked me.

can i use the bathroom? sure i said.

about 10 minutes later my ex got jumpy....go see what he's up to in there

i knocked on the door lester yeh wait a minute LESTER i pulled the unlocked door open. there was lester sitting on the can with a huge spike in his hand trying to find a vein. i snatched it away from him in disgust. please please he pleaded i'm sick. being, of late, in similar circumstances myself i returned the works whispering but let's make it look good for the chick sure he whimpered **all right** i shouted **clean up & get the hell out of here & never come back....**soon he reemerged scratching & stoned said thanks & split.

after that incident lester disappeared. i, nor anyone else, had seen him for months. it was rumored that he had found some rich old lady uptown & was shacking up with her. then the news came down to me from bob, lester's best & maybe only real friend. lester had O.D.ed & was taken to bellevue for treatment. after his recovery he was acting really strange so the doctors got permission to keep him a couple of weeks for observation. about 3 days after he was admitted he was found hanged by his belt in his room. they said it was suicide. til this day i wonder....

lester had talent. lester was young.

A SUPERINTENDENT'S EYES #31
(war dream)

i found myself on the ground floor   in a small room
of a big blding
in short sleeves (in a BIG blding) with a white rabbit
sleeping under the bed

the quilt was a faded grey patchwork

outside the garbage cans stood in a perfect line
just as i had left them
all 7 were empty

the day was a sad haiku

A SUPERINTENDENT'S EYES #32
(will guy)

you know what the trouble with me & you is, will — we don't know how to get ahead — & we're not good at being failures either. we're hungry but not starving. you with the cockroaches & cat shit — me with the dust chipped paint & useless collectibles. children of the 50's & 60's respectively. we both fought the second american civil war. only problem is we fought ourselves more than anyone else. we emerged disenchanted, battle scarred & somewhat less than victorious. me wanting too much — you not wanting enough. you see, will, it's like we stopped somewhere along the way & have kind of given up but not really — yet even when we fool ourselves into believing we've begun the journey again it's usually just another trip around the block. & what makes it all so frustrating is that you sort of feel that it's all o.k. & maybe just maybe you're right. & as i still fight you look at me lovingly wearing your ascot & your wide brimmed hat & say

stop wanting so much already stop wanting.

A SUPERINTENDENT'S EYES #33
(jony)

i made a big mistake kissing jony goodbye at the class reunion. i hadn't seen him in 25 years & our opening hugs were filled with genuine hardiness. but when it came time to leave he bent toward me where i sat & i leaned upward & planted a small glancing kiss on his sweaty cheek. he arched back suddenly stood quite erect & with the outer edge of his right hand wiped my kiss away & smiled a polite "not likely" smile when i told him to call whenever he was in town.

he had been my closest friend at the close of the 8th grade. they (his really eccentric family) lived in the biggest house on their block & kept a "negro" blues musician in their garage. he apparently did light chores around the place & was at that time the only person of color in the neighborhood. their house however was always a mess.

jony & his wife had traveled all the way from the west coast to this tiny school in brooklyn...his wife actually remarking, kind of snooty like, that they had given up a trip to the riviera to be here.

"what are you doing with yourself?" i queried. "my mother always wanted me to be a doctor so i became a doctor. & you?"
"nothing." i said "my mother didn't want me to be anything. so i became nothing."

A SUPERINTENDENT'S EYES #34
(half life)

"they've taken ½ my life" he said in a thin pale voice. the room's colors were changing as the day was ending. "it's gone." he muttered sweeping his right foot shyly across the rug in a semi-circle like a kid who got caught doing some thing. a low wind climbed the sill & lifted the top off a small pile of ashes that sat in the corner of the now darkening room. he reached for the lamp which was too far away, the mattress cushioning his thigh. the ashes resettled about the room. his mouth felt like a parched hallway. his eyes a scorched page. in some other place he had once slept deeply...drugged...until small fires woke him licking his soles with their heat. now their ashes are with him wherever he seeks rest & every yawn is like a fierce wind & every word a flame...there is not one face in the darkness that can console him & that part of his life which was consumed can no longer bear witness to what was.

horse dies
car dies
windmill turns
  around

A SUPERINTENDENT'S EYES #35
(spring street)

spring street starts on the bowery
& stops at the hudson
or vice versa

i turned down spring st.
from the bowery
toward the hudson
on my way home
turned the other way
as i saw you in turn
turn
your eyes turning away

the little girl said to her mother
— help me help me i'm drowning —
reaching out her arm body leaning toward the curb

drowning on spring street
between the bowery
& the hudson

it is late winter or early spring
depending on how
you look at it

we dump our garbage
all over this island of dreams

& borrow what we can
walking
always
walking

you turn i turn

spring st. starts & stops

i always end up somewhere in between

A SUPERINTENDENT'S EYES #36
(dead lips)

she kissed me. i had turned & walked back toward her only out of a sense of duty so as not to hurt her feelings. & to supply her with a body for her momentarily overflowing affection.

she put her hands on my forearms & kissed me 3 times.

Dead Lips   she said sweetly   Dead Lips

in the field
a 3 legged dog
forms the late autumn
landscape

A SUPERINTENDENT'S EYES #37
(the spot)

1. my mother*

today i found out that they found
a spot on my mother's liver
a small red spot
lava flow / receding beach
the afternoon sun on my winter day
a small spot that curses   stains
ruins my mother's liver's life
i see red   on red
stare at the door of this tiny apt.
& pretend there is no door
in my mouth blue prisoners
sing
my yawn sleeps inside her
my mourning is premature
yet just
time served is taken away
like an unfinished meal
i live in what i believe
live in the wings
in some part of what i still
believe
& disappear thru an exit
that i pretend is no longer there

* my mother has since passed on.

plates shift
unsettling the tissue
a new lake appears
whole islands are swallowed up
& spit out
new mountains rise
cracks form suddenly & just as suddenly
are sealed
this street is as crowded as any major highway
crowded with the promise of
escape.

2. his mother

"who killed your mother?" – "CANCER" – "where is he?
i'm gonna shoot him in the face. 1 gun. 1 bullet. in the face."

A SUPERINTENDENT'S EYES #38
(bitter cold)

as i entered the post office, a scabrous, half toothless man in his 30's, who seemed to be holding the inner door open for everyone, said, "spare some change?" i ignored him thinking "scrounge" yet feeling the usual obligatory guilt.

i dropped my letter into the airmail slot, turned my collar up & turned to leave hoping he would no longer be there. but when i heard an exotic female voice wafting thru the air with an ever so polite thank you, i knew that he was. i stuffed my paws in my pockets & made my descent.

when i reached him, i debated quickly with myself about using another door (i don't mind holding the door but hate having it held for me.) & so i did. my mind shifted images in micro seconds & in those same seconds he noticed & had the other door open & waiting for me.

i walked by him hurriedly, eyes down, mumbling, "don't do this all day. it ain't worth it."

midway down he said in a drowsy, half drunk voice "as long as the beer keeps flowing."

opening the outer door   the bitter wind
ripened my sleeping cheeks

A SUPERINTENDENT'S EYES #39
(another long ride)

1.

"remember you could be like that" i say
pointing to the seat just vacated by the young man
with the soft beige face
his shoes   his socks   his coat   all ripped
his hair mangled by the many materials of life
but strangely
a sad soft sensitive sanity
still lingered amongst his desperation
still lingers now
in the empty seat
opposite

the subway doors close.

2.

i don't pay attention to the plants hanging in my front window in my tiny overcrowded apt. but i've always wanted them there. it's the "intellectual thing." i used to have two worn & splintered exposed wood floors now one is covered by a drab grey indoor outdoor carpet i took from a vacated apt. & the other by black linoleum tiles speckled with white that have never been cared for properly & therefore are dull, cracking & becoming unglued. my wife is a stolen angel. a myth of heavy

indulgence. how can indulgence be anything else
but.......

i ride alone in this midday crowd late at night in the
early morning on a windy
afternoon sweating.......i think about my plants....

life is red sometimes....

3.

& me stuck in the blues........in this teeny little
square....this scribble that juts & turns
& stops.....i'm sad but "cultured".......self taught clammy
cluttered & short.....
poor but not that poor.....

the subway doors open.

A SUPERINTENDENT'S EYES #40
(dream — the time tuner)

we're leaning against a large grey stone loft blding & she says to me would you rather be dead or go into a time tuner...i think hand on chin...dead or time tuner...well dead i guess, thinking of the cosmic possibilities or the possible cosmic loneliness of being stuck inside a time tuner...oh i don't know. maybe both i reconsider thinking of the w.c. fields line "I'd rather be in Philadelphia."

SCENE CHANGE:

we're in a good sized room where i turn on a rather large tv
the show The Prisoner is on.
the episode is called The Time Tuner.
well the Prisoner wants to escape.
he finds himself on a desolate street in front of the columned entrance to the underground (subway to us). he sees seated slumped on the steps a young man wearing a wrinkled off white shirt & blue dungarees head in hands...as the Prisoner approaches the young man raises his head & slowly rising turns ½ way toward the Prisoner but then turns again & rushes down the steps. the Prisoner follows. the young man runs thru a narrow archway onto the railway platform. turns left. the Prisoner follows. turns right. the platform is very bright. the train is pulling in. the blue & white tiles of the platform become animated (as in cartoon). the train which is pulling in fast also becomes animated. so does the bright light of the station. across the top of the train window where

the destination should be are the words *TIME TUNER*. the train is silver. sleek. streamlined. the doors open. the young man enters the middle door of the middle car. the Prisoner enters the front door of same. young man sits. Prisoner stands near door that leads into next car. the doors close. train quickly, quietly pulls out. the prisoner grasps the hand strap. there is a smattering of people on the train. all this time i, the unwilling observer in this dream, feel uneasy about the young man...thinking that he is a spy for the "other" side & that he is leading the Prisoner into a trap. an announcer comes on the address system & says in a sweet (young irish catholic american) voice (probably has dirty blond hair) very relaxed... *"WELCOME to the TIME TUNER...you may think you've escaped something...death perhaps...by coming here...but that is not necessarily so...see that old man over there...*(camera focuses on lonely old guy... *"he thinks he's escaped death by coming here...that woman* (camera scans to ugly broken toothed woman losing her unkempt hair) *killed her husband & escaped here with her lover rather than face her punishment..."*

pan to her lover on the opposite side of the car:

& at the end of the seat the young man (spy) with no one in between him & her lover.

(all the people are real though the train itself is still animated)...

"......& that young man over there" the announcer says....................................i wake up

A SUPERINTENDENT'S EYES #41
(late night)

i get horny for my wife. she's in the kitchen reading a newspaper. she doesn't respond. so i go into the bedroom & put on tv all day long i've been cleaning out the basement. again! the late night talk show host is interviewing a pretty model in a tight black dress & showing us her swimsuit photos in a popular magazine.

she'd rather go into business than acting she says...i sigh with relief...cut to a commercial.

swedish meatball dog food...the accent is decidedly foreign.

the next guest is an anal juggling comedian. juggles wonder bread, hard rubber balls, ice cream & raw liver........my horniness goes away.

commercial...i get up to pee.

............last guest arrives...talks about his visit to a trojans factory. says 1.1 million are made a day every day. the host asks ...does that mean that's how many are bought & used each day?

........probably...he replies........ he then goes on to add that the place is run by an ex navy officer who always refers to the product as "the goods."

"the goods" are tested by women who pick them up with their hands. some using one hand. some using two. they are stretched over penis shaped rods & then dunked into water. this is done to test their strength & check for leaks...if passed they are packaged & shipped out.

my wife has entered the bedroom
& now lies
next to me in bed.
she has taken off her robe.
she is naked under the covers.

the right side of my neck stiffens.
i get up & go into the kitchen.

A SUPERINTENDENT'S EYES #42
(the day begins)

my coat is on i'm ready to leave the house suddenly my stomach feels heavy loose like i'm going to spill my guts out any second...i rush to the toilet pull off my coat throw it on the floor pull down my pants & sit on the pot...panicked & in pain...i squeeze & squeeze but nothing comes out. i get up pull up my pants pick up my coat leave the house lock the door & hit the street.

it is mid-march   the wind is   rushing around corners

A SUPERINTENDENT'S EYES #43
(lines, fingers, birth, fags)

the check cashing joint is full. it's friday
payday
the line increases & decreases
just like at the fancy art opening last night
the place packed with has-beens & wannabes
stuck in the pangs & pages of a coming & going generation
no longer innocent
filling the air with a dense impermanent presence

the computer breaks down
i break with the line
& break wind in the breathing world

the moon has four fingers
& moves thru our window
with poise
the rats have attacked the garbage
at least twice today
yet we still die upon a lover's kiss

my wife & i walk alone
thru the weekend streets
dreaming of chow dogs
& skulls.

my brother got to see my mother pregnant twice. my sister got to see her pregnant once. today on the phone my mother told me that the pump they put in her liver makes her look pregnant. i will try to see her before summer's end.

i look at fags with disdain & curiosity. with a bit of longing.
always threatened.
the storm is passing   the weather carries itself further east.

someone calls my name on the street. we stand awhile &
talk of nothing important.
it is getting time to rekindle old friendships
why not?

"Cupid draw back your Bow..........."

A SUPERINTENDENT'S EYES #44
(the bard, ingestion)

sun visors up on his glasses
the black man
talks to himself

hot bright day
bottle in hand

"Anyone can read Shakespeare.
Ask New York University.
He can read Shakespeare. But she can't."

pointing randomly at people

"It's simple. Anyone can do it.
Shakespeare had no wife.
Never even had a woman.
A man can read Shakespeare
but a woman can't.
If the woman read it   he kill her.
Anyone can read Shakespeare.
Ask the universities.
Shakespeare. Nothin' hard about that."

the truck driver unloading his van says   AMEN.

we eat   & eat   & eat
we talk & talk   & talk

chew chicken bones & steak   vegetables & salad

the cemetery is so quiet   the wind in the trees
tears my wife in half

there is a moment of beauty   a cloud moving east
her face   & then   the close up

there's something too big here   too out of place   too real

EXIT

A SUPERINTENDENT'S EYES #45
(the strangers)

there are strange new people entering my building.
opening the door.
there's a soft grey drizzle outside
beginning to slip thru history. humidity.
believe it or not strangers are appearing.
strange new people going in & out.
opening the door.
closing the door.
the heat makes exits on my shoulders & brow   like x's
crosses
exits my underarms.
harpies caught in fan blades   laugh at my desires
coveting my frustrations.

my heart beats like a door
closing & opening.

there are strange new people entering my premises

my very private premises.

the day is pale & sticky   like my skin.

A SUPERINTENDENT'S EYES #46
(lumber)

the drum & bass pound upward thru the floor
from the shoe store below
they permeate every pore of my apt.
as well as every pore of my skin
even as i shower

morning til night
drum & bass
& shoes

one of the girls in apt. 13 is moving out today
actually she's been moving out for about a week now
mainly on the weekends

as a gift for my never having had any contact with them
she & her now former roommate
have left me plenty of waste to remove
come next garbage night
including about 100 4 by 4's
full of nails

at least when i carry them out
i'll have
all that "good" music
to accompany me

i hope the evening will be a clear one

A SUPERINTENDENT'S EYES #47
(closer to dying)

thank god you shit & sweat   she tells me
this probably keeps you alive

                i smell so bad from beneath my underarms
                these days

        where are they all these flying things
        when all that rain comes
                down

                                inside like us   i say

my smell slipping out of me onto the lawn.

A SUPERINTENDENT'S EYES #48
(liberation)

1.

i am facing the watchtower. 10:26 pm. 76 degrees. no moon in this direction. couples on either side of me. i am at the helm. i think of jumping in. the water looks cold. it is night water. with light on it. rippling & swirling & churning. it is like water described many time before. but that one mystery spot moves faster than the rest. a sphere of loneliness. there is a loud singing pounding against my back. a wordless song. an encore at the beginning. i turn & bow. i turn again. dismiss the air. i think of jumping in.

after the applause   i walk away

2.

my wife & i are on the train in the rain
all the seats are occupied by singles
imagine what it would be like
to open Ed's Auto Collision every morning

the rain increases   next stop last stop then 3 days at the beach

single: by one's self   alone   unaccompanied

imagine opening Ed's all alone   & closing it

½ the singles were already ha(l)ves to begin with
        woman baby intimate couple pair rain

        salami   provolone   how immense i am   alone

we reach the beach   the rain concludes   the sun docks

A SUPERINTENDENT'S EYES #49
(who's horn is this...)

you see he said *i'm gettin' worried*
we're startin' to think alike

the tenor sounds a lot like sonny rollins
well the song is tenor madness

& coltrane too & ayler well more ayler than 'trane

geez i wish he'd sound more like himself if possible

the experimental psychology student wears a black long sleeved turtleneck. we sit at the front of the club. her elbows are on the table in front of me. she wears a soft smile & her teeth show at a high point in the solo. her eyes are a natural shake.

oh the women in the house
are cheeks of fresh strawberries
bows of fine spun linen
amethyst
ruby
emerald lobes
fresh unfolding flowers

i miss you because i am alone & because i miss you

there is no one else so when i'm done imagining i imagine you i am being drummed   i want my cock in your mouth

i want to grab your tits   & twist your nipples

bite your belly   grab handfuls of your arse

  i need to solo   & be soloed on
            the cheeks of the women are pale pomegranates
              & poor promises
                          the tenor is not himself tonight

      i am trying   trying   to want you..........

A SUPERINTENDENT'S EYES #50
(toilet)

my house is being destroyed. they started to build my new bathroom. i've had a tub in the kitchen & toilet in the hall for years. finally, after no pay, this job is paying off. i get a toilet inside. a big wide shower to boot.

it's the second day & the workmen have only put in an hour. now they're gone.

it's snowing. lunch break? where the hell did they go? my wife's in japan. she'll be back in a month. i hope they'll be done by then. i hope they'll be back by then. if they ever come back. will they ever come back?

i must move all these boxes to the basement until
the work is finished.
this new toilet. it's displaced my "study" & a major
clothes closet.
i guess i'll build a closet where the tub was & make
more shelves
in the living room & bedroom.
i guess the kitchen table will become my new study.

snowflowers breathe into my face
i am stuck   like the hands of 2 lovers   circling

i know my shapes
but even children   grow into wars

A SUPERINTENDENT'S EYES #51
(*the trial*)

a long time tenant & equally long time struggling actor
(who actually bought my new cd at tower records & who
has recently landed a small role in a stage adaptation of
kafka's *the trial*) introduced me to his girlfriend tonight:

"This is Steve   our resident poet..."

i say "What he means to say is... This is Steve, our resident
superintendent & an incompetent one at that but he doesn't
want to embarrass me...Nice to meet you..."

"You too" she replies.   i get on my bike & pedal away.

riding eastward on a narrow street to catch a late night set
i wonder to myself as i maneuver against the traffic

"Who's Life Am I Really Taking In My Hands"

the moon races   with me

A SUPERINTENDENT'S EYES #52
(thinning foliage)

i'm waiting here for almost nothing
my shadow waits outside
i sell my soul much too cheaply
my name is in the waves
in the waiting room
in monotones

assumption
hypothesis
experimentation

so immersed in my fluids
in the late morning
air

the movements of jump rope ghosts
linger

a few voices linger on the branches

will i ever be done   sweeping these leaves?

A SUPERINTENDENT'S EYES #53
(i hear sleeping...)

like berryman said too many of us have been born....if i had it to do over again i wouldn't. not today anyway. it was the first big snow & i spent quite some time shoveling & salting down the sidewalk. if i did repeat this process, like snowfall, there'd probably be very little difference.

the big jowly woman at the table opposite me is saying something about sex & morning to the man she's with. the tunes coming over the restaurant speakers all sound familiar except they're sung in Vietnamese. the pavement out front has been breathed clean of its gift of snow.

i hear sleeping
& i know it's jump off time
i'm a wrapped piano
strapped & jacketed
waiting
to be rocked

a superintendent's eyes #54
(prose & cons)

as i passed the derelict i could almost smell the holes in his body. he walked at what is euphemistically called "a snail's pace" on what is commonly known as a "crisp, clear" winter afternoon. he wore an old khaki moth-eaten military coat & slung over his shoulder was what one would generally term a neatly tied "bundle of rags." his beard was salt & pepper. his skin, for easy accessing, black.

right after becoming a "fountain pen," they couldn't decide whether to sedate me or give me shock treatment. they opted for both. (i needed neither.) it was my first real experience with drugs but not with electricity. i already had a tv a record player & a lamp. maybe my "madness" was all due to that older uncircumcised boy with the big dick making fun of my cleaner smaller circumcised one when we were having sex with those two girls in the basement of the only apartment building on the block. it was a grey afternoon after school, we were smoking marlboros & the girls were facing the grey concrete wall, naked. we were all naked. standing up. i wish i had a video of that day. or even a photo to make it more real.

i wish i knew how many people were taking pictures along 5th avenue on this clear, crisp dionysian afternoon. i've counted a couple so far & more than twice that many holes.

maybe it was the time my dog blackie fell backwards down the cellar stairs & broke his back after my cat whitey spooked him. i had just gotten done walking him…sweet gentle black cocker spaniel...they had to put him to sleep…i still lose sleep over it. i was very young. i wish i had a photo of him. or of that moment. i loved him. i really did. i think i stopped loving after that. i mean in the real sense...i started feeling guilty about everything even the things i didn't do. paranoia set in. my self consciousness disease started blossoming. i became so moody. threw temper tantrums constantly...started smoking & hanging out with the kid with the big dick & those 2 girls…met my third girlfriend. did all kinds of perverted shit with her. we were finally broken up after 3 years on the advice of my shrink. did better in school. got shock & sedation. taken out of school. eventually got put away & started taking drugs. dropped out never ever dropped back in...wouldn't couldn't. started counting holes & will never stop. i wish i had photos of all these............

h Oles

A SUPERINTENDENT'S EYES #55
(history)

i have memory of the thing
though i was not there
i see it clearly in my mind
though it may never have occurred
a continuous obsessive nagging of event
all the pieces relayed to me
by various participants

joy & the lack
of
substance

i am the last drop of unseeded semen
on the tip of my cock

like the collective memory of raindrops
& the mud that forms
after they fall

i too am mud
i too........revolution.

men in prison
VIDEO CASSETTE

VIDEO CASSETTE
men in prison
men in prison

A SUPERINTENDENT'S EYES #56
(r.p.m.)

revolution:

the way things go a round

act of spinning

revolve around each other choosing to or not
are revolted revolting against

turn revolutionary per matter of WORLD

stringing matters constant ephemera

continuous states

short term memory.

A SUPERINTENDENT'S EYES #57
(a bitter pill)

when the newcomer asked me where he could find an ATM machine i pointed to the ROCK STAR & said "Him. He's an ATM machine." where upon the ROCK STAR stated... "Never call anyone an ATM machine." "That's what friends are for." i said drily, immediately realizing that we weren't really friends. later that day i relayed the story to an acquaintance of both mine & the ROCK STAR'S...he said "You should never call anyone an ATM machine...especially him." whereupon i said "Well that's what friends are for." whereupon he replied "You mean friend's are supposed to bug you?" "Something like that" immediately regretting having opened my mouth in the first place.

which reminds me of something i said to someone today in the Bowery Garden when i saw one turtle mounting another from behind...... "Do you think they're "doin" it or do you think he's just happy to see her?"

it's hot outside
it's hot inside

i swallow a handful of quarters knowing that eventually
the meter will run out

A SUPERINTENDENT'S EYES #58
(wet dream — charley varrick's goodbye kiss)

"...if you can't do that, Jimmy Dick, what good are you?"

a. Nadine had been shot in the holdup. history revealed that she would not make it. "goddamn she jammin" he thought as they pulled up onto a desolate patch of countryside in order to change vehicles. "Goodbye Nadine" he said as Harman spread the powder around. "Harman cease & desist. I'll finish that up later. Go & open the other sack." Harman complied. "Oh lord" he shouted "Oh lord…like money money… money. I reckon those white fish still be swimmin'." "Hold it. Somethin' stinks here." Charley said. "Somethin' smells like a tax free sales week. Smells like money to be laundered. Whoremonger money. Drug money. Mafia money. Designer money. Over-serviced money. Uncomfortable, dirty money."

He picked up the powder bag & walked back to the car. "Goodbye Nadine. Goodbye my hard hard crop duster girl." & kissed her softly on the lips. The blood gushed from her side like herbal tea. As she reached for him, her body went limp. She was gone. He kissed her again slowly removing the wedding ring from her finger. "Goodbye Nadine" he said, pouring the remainder of the powder over her & shutting the door. He stuffed a rag in the gas tank & ignited it. He & Harman jumped in the van & left. This was not quite as hard as it sounds. When found, Nadine's body was burnt beyond recognition…like a piece of dry whole wheat toast. Only her dental records remained as proof of her short hard life.

(insert yawn)

b. “never fucked on a round bed” i say to the amazonian woman. “like boxing the compass.” “let’s try south by south-west.” she murmurs over my head. my wife is in the other room. the party is in full swing. i begin banging my crotch against her tightly clad body. she begins complaining about the young man who spurned her earlier in the evening. “you’ll find someone else.” i say absently, grunting. “in fact, there’s a kid in the other room who’s been eyeing you all night.” pounding harder & harder. with this she thrusts her knee squarely into my dick. my hardon soars & my jissum roars. “he’s crazy about you.” i moan as i come in my baby blue boxers beneath my thick black denim jeans...i wake with an AHHHHHH on my lips & her voice in my head singing “throw me over in the clover. lay me down & roll me over. & do it again. oh do it again.”

i find myself lying face down in a puddle — eyes filled with sky

post script: heaven if i’m on the guest list o.k.
if i have to pay
to get in
i’m
not
going.

A SUPERINTENDENT'S EYES #59
(anticipating the drill)

when i was young i read all the right books. i was sure that if i tried hard enough they would help me cope with my dilemma. my feelings of gross inadequacy, lack of identity & paranoia. well they did.

kafka taught me that it was ok to be a cockroach in a castle & to hate my father. camus taught me that it was fine to feel left out, floating, not remembering my mom's birthday or even the day she died. was it yesterday or today?

i was made to feel good, yet always on trial, when committing certain crimes like shoplifting. even MURDER...old fyodor, for instance, said cool, gamble, gamble all you want — so what if some of the side effects cause you to be a sick, spiteful, jealous man? yet ever so "CATHOLIC."

geez. i devoured them all. all those guidebooks for the unguideable. & look at me now. i'm a plague in a penal colony constantly rolling that rock up a hill. a mess. a boni fide mess. & proud of it. trashing everyone as i take out the trash leaving a trail of schmutz wherever i go.

ginsberg taught me that it was ok to tell america to go fuck itself. burroughs said it was ok to shoot dope. kerouac, bukowski, said fine Drink drink DrInK yourself to death. just listen to some good music along the way. or do like hemingway & just plain blow your brains out. sartre said it was all well & good to lock one's self in a small room & retch your everlovin' guts out....

diderot said it was all written up yonder anyway.

so here i am: a self-hating, self-pitying, self-medicated, selfishly cockeyed optimist. a nihilist with a fist in his too big mouth, full of existential angst, carrying around a NEGATIVE EGO the size of the grand cool guy damn always competing for last place....sick to my stomach every time i hear a gunshot or a bird chirp.

here ***I*** *be the ultimate source book on what ails me & how to make things worse...a map of bad feelings with directions on how to get to & acquire more of the same. MUCH MORE. proudly suffering & worrying always about the paranoids that are chasing Me.*

here you find a handbook on how to deal with rejection, alienation, introspection & extermination.....don't fight THEM...let THEM in. let THEM fester & grow & make you feel as uncomfortable as can be. NEVER EVER learn to accept or enjoy THEM.
i'm an unending compendium of ill will. a malcontent
i sing i bark i contort.

ME *— a survival kit for the 21st Century... a misguided miscreant who believes in the ONE SPECTACULAR god...of Masochism & Sloth....*

I, *the ignorant elitist, ill at ease Solitary Man, thank you all from the bottom of my rotting soul....* ***I,*** *who still have no idea of who i am, give thanks to all my gurus in this the worst of TIMES. i the grateful student of all who have reinforced, increased & made my* **PAIN** *o.k. & my time on this planet a bit more uneasy... thank you for helping me into my depression...for permitting me to wallow in my discomfort...for helping the myth to bare fruit....*

Hey MOM i'm O.K. Hey DAD Hey Jim Hey Bruno send in those naked dancing zombies...i am the puzzle with the missing pieces. an infinity of annotated listings. the mangled sum of all your parts...i smile as i turn the other cheek...& embrace you as i light the match....

A SUPERINTENDENT'S EYES #60
(the 48th ronin)

abraham,
(my not very biblical boss),
who, besides being the landlord,
is a bigwig real estate lawyer,
had disciplinary proceedings
instituted against him
recently

3 separate charges
of professional misconduct
in three separate cases
(all of which seemed to stem from greed)
were brought against
him

fucking with escrow without authorization
simultaneously defending clients with different interests
orchestrating bogus transfer of assets

he (the respondent) was found guilty
& his motions consistently denied
& the judges all concurred that suspension was too good

he was as a result disbarred
frankie said he did all this because he has BALLs
i said he was just stupid

now he's thinking about selling the blding*

as i sat in the restaurant the other cold winter night
with my big simmering bowl of
NABEYAKI UDON
i thought
"this is what it must have felt like
to be a samurai
without a MASTER."

** he has since signed the blding over to his daughter — frankie has long disappeared.*

A SUPERINTENDENT'S EYES #61
(white bucks)

we used to say
that anyone who wore white bucks
was a fag
they belonged to frats   were very ivy league
now those folks are married men with kids
they're doctors in connecticut
or lawyers on long island
or some kind of computer somethings
they stroll down streets where
guys who never wore white bucks hang out
tryin' to earn a buck whatever way they can
where guys who used to wear white bucks
would never have dreamed of strolling
til now

we never dressed ivy league
never knew fraternities
only knew ourselves
or so we thought
the latest hit on the jukebox
& a safe spot to sing sweet songs
on the soft side of the street

& did we sing our hearts out

some of us got lucky
& achieved success without degrees

& some luckier still
to hang out on sharp corners   under blue moons
observing   still
singing those songs

postscript:

    we used to dance at different parties
    with the same girls
    had the same names & similar dreams
    saw the same things   differently
    or totally different things

i work & live in a blding where half the occupants are gay
my apt. is directly above a shoe store...most of us wear the
same black shoes.

A SUPERINTENDENT'S EYES #62
(why not ticket the trees)

this morning i got a ticket for not separating the trash from the recyclables.
hey, i'm not responsible for what goes on in the street between midnight & dawn.

a couple of weeks ago they gave me one for all those fallen ginko leaves.
i spent the rest of the day pasting them back onto their branches.

late afternoon

a cloud-colored 1/2 moon
windswept

A SUPERINTENDENT'S EYES #63
(wisdom, magic & salt)

1.

i don't like bad guys on either side, he said, but at least if one shot you you'd know you'd be dying. the night crept cautiously around him. his eyes swelled with anger & excitement. maybe right then & there he'd explode from the magic of it all & his heavy breathing. maybe, he thought, if they'd only be more polite to each other then we'd have less problems...he started gasping for air & sinking to his knees. this at the end of that foul little triangle where thompson street meets canal.

2 cops hung there watching the shirtless boys shoot hoops. as he fell downward his head hit the pavement & his 2 hands dropped from his throat.....if only   if only

2.

in the refinement of place in the soft bellied notes that blossom from the thick fertile corpse of the land in the affirmation that i am still here though my body does not want to carry me my soft agitated fists only want to smash windshields & feel the godfucking wind...this is shallow fact & nothing else...hey you you there with the pushcart with the big square wooden wheels...sweet talk me out of here...haul me the hell out of HERE...carry me to my conclusion...& you there in the chair beside me don't rub your perfume in my face......don't ease your way into my lap....

in the refinement of this place in the quick thinking of a
good teacher
Lot & Thoth will unite will count
letters learning wisdom magic & salt

when i own a club
all the glasses
will be
plastic.

A SUPERINTENDENT'S EYES #64
(attaining great heights)

1. cleaning the drains on the roof

say alert   ALERT   stay alert i swear i'm in a state of change

it's early dammit   icy & early   my ears   my ears
must have been delivered to the wrong address
i'm winding down   now
i'd bet my glass education on it

a process of social consciousness is being designed
in the thin snapping air
it's early dammit   don't look down
plunging   plunging   my eyes are
snapping in the thin cold air
there is no sound in here
though i listen & stretch & pick myself up

the string snaps   the water flows
this was always the wrong address   stay warm.

2. backing down from the challenge

store owner east's husband knocks on my door tells me that water is leaking into his store from the ledge outside apt. 2. one such leak damaged lots of stuff in the store as well as the basement. it is a ledge that can be accessed & walked on easily through the kitchen window. i tell him i don't have a key to the apt. that we should ask the landlord or his daughter if they do. as it turns out the landlord's not available & we can't reach the daughter. so i tell him that i'll get a ladder & go into the side yard & see what i can do.   i'm now in the eastern side yard beneath apt. 2's ledge. the western side yard is where the garbage is kept. the snow is up to my waist. i put the ladder against the blding. he gets agitated "get up there & clean the snow." i start my ascent & suddenly freeze stating that the ledge is too high. that i am too little, that it is way too cold & the snow on the ground too deep. we scream & scream at each other. then the landlord's younger daughter arrives. she doesn't have a key either. she starts screaming at me now. telling me how lazy & inefficient i am. "it's leaking into the clothes store. hurry up." by this time the husband who is a 7 foot millionaire cowboy type tells me that it's my job & i should keep going. i start my ascent again, freeze up again & begin to groan like a sick puppy..."i can't do this. it's too high. i'm afraid & besides i don't get paid to do this. do it yourself." "you're the super that's your job." they scream. "fuck you — fuck you" — i yell — losing my grip plunging into a snow drift below. the cowboy (whom i've never gotten along with) suddenly comes to my rescue. helps me up. takes the shovel while angrily telling me how incompetent i am & scurries up the ladder in his new cowboy boots & expensive jeans clears the snow & proceeds to crack the ice beneath.

since then the ledge has been re-tarred. we get along fine or i should say not at all. he even tips occasionally. particularly when i shovel snow from the front of their store.

water flows — there's a snapping in the thick cold air —
this was the wrong address — always has been the wrong address

A SUPERINTENDENT'S EYES #65
(the dreams that end responsibilities)

1. acid trip

i walked back to the blding in the high snow   pants rolled up   bare feet   they told me to do it i said   they told me to do it......you're seeing things i see nothing i see try to see things my way i can't see a thing   you just don't get it....2 merciful eyes in the wood behind the moon red merciful eyes they told me to do it they did they really did.....

2. men working above

today the sky is blue how many times before have i said that the sun is fully bright & as near as danger i am moving so i have been told many times before by science 2 men are high up on the scaffold pointing the brick emitting bright red dust all over the sidewalk i'm as high as one can be without wings as low as the thinnest clouds softly randomly clawing by i need not wear a suit or sail this close to the ground again on 2 feet rented how many times have i told you this about myself in this actor city from my sky so close to the ground the sparkle tone of your actress voice calling thru the traffic a radio of love that creates motion warm on my skin

the day is a book of photos   big clumsy   turned by the wind

i hear you   though you are like the absence of birds

A SUPERINTENDENT'S EYES #66
(emergencies)

1.

if you don't have a true emergency return a gift to wildlife. there's no better way. don't give up even if life is pressing you. but please talk to psychics not to me unless it's an emergency.

2.

blue curacao spilled on my sneaker & stuck to its rim & seeped thru the canvas onto my skin as i stepped over the gaunt man lying against the lamp-post to get a peek at the action inside the bodega. blue curacao splashed onto my generic high tops when my careless foot hit the bottle at the gaunt man's feet sending it spinning & rolling toward the curb.

BLUE SKIN *i think now*
BLUE DISEASE

his frail arm lifted beckoning toward his mouth...
"i don't smoke" i whispered leaning down toward him......
right foot falling fast asleep.

3.

when i transferred my pen from my pants to my shirt i hadn't noticed that it had leaked. when i took it from my shirt i found small blue inkstains scattered along the entire bottom of my shirt pocket & one large stain along the shoulder. i had been carrying the shirt balled up. i was riding in a hot subway car & would occasionally unfurl my shirt to wipe my sweat away. particularly on my face. i was sweating much more than usual. i wore my bathing suit under my pants. she told me that i had blue all over my face. i tried to wipe it away with a tissue. this made things worse. we were headed to my brother's house on Long Island. a rare visit. the ink had smeared miserably. i now had about six blotches on my face as big as oversized freckles. i stopped rubbing & thought of the Nathaniel Hawthorne story as i stared at the birth mark on my wife's right cheek. it was sunday. i was headed for the beach instead of making money. my shirt, it seemed, was ruined. my face hopefully was not. my wife, touching a small sore on her forearm looked at my "freckles" & proclaimed:

"it's amazing — huh — we all have this healing power."

A SUPERINTENDENT'S EYES #67
(small pressures stapled to my forklift tongue)

1. retreat from fascism

when i put this old black shirt on i said to myself nice shirt —
how come nobody ever says "hey steve, that's a nice
shirt"?

well tonight tom said "NICE SHIRT" looking up at me
from the bottom of the stairs.
"thanks i think it's a nice shirt too...." then i told him that i
wondered why nobody
ever said before — hey steve, that's a nice shirt..................

2. judgment (inside the law)

the cowbell rings. it's feeding time at the courthouse. i am
here to plead my case. i look at each judge's face as they
emerge from their tiny rooms. old. young. soft. cold. warm.
hard. white. black. red. tan. which one will judge me. the
bell rings again. i am too hungry to eat.
morning light steals thru the windows
my stomach leaks out of the bottom of my shoes
& spreads across the floor

3. democratization

this hot urban afternoon the riders & paramedics open —
winged one
toward the slow light

"if you can't come with me don't fool with my meat. if
you're dancing for pleasure think of the others who
can't..........sometimes."

hot urban inner china new world cracked ceiling
the natural stuff area codes along this stretch
the characters
franco-italian crystals frescoes of dark eyes
hispanic indians
at work in this village of beasts & breasts

i sing with impure heart
my love my hate so strong
they hoist my moving heart up toward the crossbeams
a man aweight in treason & treasure
my bones slowly returned to me

i go from my mother's house to the clouds. they no longer
block the sun. the words made bone. i would gladly give
my bones for them. i have done my running for today.

A SUPERINTENDENT'S EYES #68
(bone boy's holiday)

1. the personals:

bone boy bares bones seeks job

the idea is to surround one's self w/books

a night @ IRVING PLAZA
simon stands @ the periphery of the MOSHING
bone boy holds the microphone this close to his teeth
barely breathing gives *Thanks*

this will be our last show in a long time thank you
n.y. ARE YOU READY

i bare my bones she flirts from the stage
bone boy pours water on his head
she hurls insults @ no one in particular
(it is in the nature of their song)
the idea is to surround one's self with:

liars expatriots & thugs
boy bares bones
microphone in throat
off-stage wanna-be-thugs
just names
& how far a name can carry

but name is not thug **bone boy** carries himself
into the garden

throws himself into the crowd
the show is nearly over simon almost against his will
gets caught up in the moshing
the show ends   off stage she hurls insults
@ no one in particular
flirts with the crowd   the screen shuts down
backstage is business as usual
i clench my privilege into a fist
and stuff it into my pocket
bone boy hurls himself from the balcony lands in simon's lap
simon smiles laughs   brushes off the splinters   goes home
his trophy is resistance
his failure is loyalty   **bone boy seeks job**   the idea is

2. a black hole:

teeth held together by wind   boy's mouth become black hole
pins rattling the palate >   *why everyone get sick?*
why everyone die?

boy's words like hollow tin   *why's everyone in such a hurry?*

for 7 hrs bone boy wanders the corridors the waiting rooms
fill with language & accident shackled prisoners in orange
frocks arrive invisible & are marched into a secret room
the letters   *DOC*   inscribed on their backs *(do they think*
alike?)   **BIG WHITE LETTERS > DOC.**   *am i*
sick? save me. will i die?
what's the hurry?
after 7 hrs bone boy wanders out into the cold dark street
words rattle thru the hole that is his mouth rise in the wind
we're almost home feet. we're almost home. & almost is
better than faraway.
he swallows my breath. *the chairs were so hard. the day*
has only just begun.

A SUPERINTENDENT'S EYES #69
(morning to sunset)

1. morning

it had been raining all night & i was worried. i promised yuko a day of walking in the sun in search of signs of spring. away from this neighborhood. i awake & walk into the kitchen.

drinking morning tea
rain
on the window ledge

after breakfast we settle down & try to accept our fate. it rains & rains. the cats sleep. we listen to music. write. read. sudden thunder. twitching. everything clean for spring.
i decide to mop the halls.

by early afternoon the rain finally stops & the streets rapidly dry under a strong spring sun. we prepare for our walk. the halls are clean. the streets are too.

by the park   across the street
blackbirds   quarrel

we walk for many blocks. new buds springing up everywhere. the city, as always, sustaining itself. we walk & walk until darkness & hunger catch up with us. the sparrow rubs its beak on a branch. a squirrel rolls around in the grass. how idyllic can things get?

"what a carefree existence they lead" my stomach grumbles

"let's go to that nice restaurant on 14th street"

she agrees & we head crosstown.

pink hyacinths @ sunset
breaking away from
themselves

we arrive at the restaurant, aptly named, SOL DE ORO,* very tired, order our favorite dishes, eat & digest the day. the food is, as usual, great. we order extra rice.

convex moon
tasting a lemon wedge
her yellow sweater

we head home filled & contented. this big city night unfolding around us.

2. sunset (sol de oro — a reprise)

god must have stopped at the sol de oro. he must be there still in this airy space on w. 14th just above 6th ave. he dwells inside the menu & the smiles of the waiters. & guides the hands of the cooks. he is perhaps the final silent partner as he picks up our tab & closes los puertos de plata por la noche.

one rainy night
he must have stopped here
filled with hunger
& after whetting his appetite
he left a golden ray on this wide back street...

& for a small price we sit at the table prepared for us &
eat until our stomachs burst
& our hearts balloon with joy

* there were similar chinese-cuban restaurants in chelsea, now, like this one, long gone as are most in manhattan.

A SUPERINTENDENT'S EYES #70
(the remnant)

when the jamaican man sheltering himself from the cold saw me entering the blding he gathered up all his possessions without a word. among them were newspapers. a crumpled paperback. a shaggy wool blanket. & many many sheets of paper. i went straight into my apt. after a few moments i walked back to the outer hall to make sure he was gone. he was.

basically he had left the hall fairly clean leaving behind only a folded scrap of paper with the following handwritten poem on it:

Camp Dream

Truly & True is Jah.
A (illegible) of Celebration in the Camp of the true
I can stay from here
That's if Iam Sure.
(illegible) hear .
The Mountain is blue
with a smoke of Incense Surrounding Truly & True is Jah.
A (illegible) of Celebration in the Camp of the true
I can stay from here
That's if Iam Sure.
(illegible) hear.
The Mountain is blue
with a smoke of Incense Surrounding
the Camp.
But only if the camp remains under strain

Once chant was true
& I mean so Blue.
for it heals all wounds.
Now it is the Camp
of the Strong
Are You so strong
Rasta Man.
Spirituality hes left
hes left your Camp
At least I believe so
Or is it still there.
Underneath A Sack cloth
of ha (illegible).

A SUPERINTENDENT'S EYES #71
(little things)

i'm always thinking about little things. like for the past few days about 3 buttons i have to buy for that corduroy jacket i got for a coupla bucks in the thrift shop. i keep singing that wretched beach boys song over & over again in my head for weeks...you know the one..."wouldn't it be nice if we were older..." etc. etc....no chance of that anymore...

walking down the dampening street i got lost in
the young chinese girl's
dark dark pony tail while thinking about the
archways on the church steeple
in the village square pregnant with bells & sky
& the statue of saint someone-i-was-too-far-
away-to-tell-who
standing below them like a mirage
as if blessing the oncoming stale evening

i laid awake most of the night thinking about the plumber that came this morning & how he'd have to wake me up early (which he did) & how i'd have to stay in the tenant's apt. with him until his job was done...& i sang that tune over & over again in my head as i crushed my ears with a heavy pillow...straining all the while to hear the faucet drip.

i thought about that gorgeous crystal inkwell i sold 10 years ago just to get an extra 10 bucks...over & over again lost in the dark pony tail of obsession.

those things that force one to be expressive & to create oneself

postscript 1 — i am caught painting the wind
instead of the windows

postscript 2 — Scotty*: a superintendent's curse
how long can i go on with someone like Scotty
stalking my peace of mind.

*Scotty the landlord's son-in-law moved to new jersey became a real upstanding guy & contractor, though for over 2 years he's promised to fix my apt. to no avail.

A SUPERINTENDENT'S EYES #72
(dropping the ball)

1. resolutions

instead of partying all night we decide — for the first time ever — to come home to watch the BALL drop. this year the mayor & a famous weirdo performer are supposed to push the "lever." the plan: finish up a few chores — get naked — get into bed. turn on the tube. watch.
we get home. all goes as planned. yuko's in the kitchen preparing soba noodles, the typical japanese meal for new year's eve. suddenly at 11:59 the tv goes black. i panic — scream hysterically — break into a cold sweat. pushing buttons. unplugging & re-plugging plugs...just as suddenly the picture returns. it's 12:01 — the ball has dropped without us. i curse. stomp. what a way to begin the new year. like the rest of my life.

doom, gloom & little cash — no room & lots of trash.

the tenants down the hall are having what seems to be a huge drunken orgy & i know that by tomorrow ½ the bottles, ½ the garbage & most of the mess will be theirs.
i flip from one channel to another maniacally hoping to catch an instant replay — past the honeymooners marathon — past an aged dick clark whose face looks like chopped liver & whose voice sounds like mud. i land on a program which like my life is in simple black & white. it's the episode of the TWILIGHT ZONE called *People Are Alike All Over* where Roddy McDowell is duped & ends up in a "comfortable" cage in a zoo on MARS. *earthlings — flimsy little 2 legged animals with extremely small heads.* small brains. evil thoughts. i return

to the kitchen grab my noodles. throw some week old chopped liver onto the plate. make my first egg cream of the new year which turns out flatter than the squashed rat in the cluttered courtyard. return to the bedroom & settle in. right then & there i begin a list of resolutions:

start a journal — lose weight — make money — be tidier — nicer — more giving — less angry — less bitter — less jealous — eat healthier — get rid of lots of junk cluttering up the apartment — spend money — speak less — learn some social skills & grace — accrue more social cultural & symbolic capital — more social mobility (which direction) — drink more fluids — be less obsessive — less compulsive — kinder — gentler — stop biting my nails — picking my nose — gnawing at my cuticles — bleed less — stop offering to give people directions — stop helping others in general — exercise more

the lever was pressed by an italian & a jew — this building was owned by italians & jews — i grew up amongst italians & jews. at the close of the year i found out that columbus was an italian jew — a prejudiced man who died in poverty never really knowing what land he had discovered — my doorbell keeps ringing — my chest (close to my heart) begins to itch — as i scratch what seems to be a maggot or a bookworm appears between my fingers — i crumple it up along with the paper i am writing on — dispose of both in the small straw wastebasket in my bedroom realizing that i have never yet kept a resolution so why start now — the tv goes fuzzy again. the sci-fi channel will always be my life. it's like spring outside. i am lucky to be loved even if it is a heavy burden to bear.

o.k. kids let's conjugate the VERBS resolve, revolt, revolve, evolve...DISSOLVE >

2. dissolves

the tv is totally broken. the light spills where it may.
i am enclosed in a room full of books. surrounded by voices –
suicides – murders – thefts – near suicides – crashes –
i am an unfriendly reminder to strangers – locked inside
my own infomercial – destined to run again with or
without the black & white with or without the color –
cable – or antenna – destined to run in this sleepy room
surrounded by fuzzy pictures.

A SUPERINTENDENT'S EYES #73
(conclusions)

1. menus

classic   is   in the word   not exotic
but a venue like noble
or post noble
the ability to be/
no bility

this is camouflage   at the end of the century

do not put that thing here
blue bag black bag clear bag broom bulb boiler
prevention is the star falling at end time

between & destined as if before the private zone
established   circuit breaker   ladder   fixture key

no trespassing   punishable by law   post no bills
prosecutors will be violated

'tis not the inevitable like HUNTING   No MeNuS   pLeAsE

nothing is permanent

2. don't shoot until......

the landlord is talking to a tenant. "it's only a matter of time. you'll see. they'll shoot down a plane & then we'll see what happens?"

i am wandering around the **NO FLY ZONE.** hauling out the garbage. hernias bulging.

"who'll shoot down a plane?" i ask. "KA DAFFY." the landlord answers.

i fire back. "who? don't you mean.....?" the landlord stammers assertively
voice like rough sandpaper...."UHUHUHUHUH"

"Hussein. Saddam Hussein" i shoot as i reach the street
sack of trash almost parallel to him & the tenant
(an israeli who works in the shoe store on the ground floor)

"right," he says. "what's the difference anyway?"

"the difference is..." i say hauling the bag to the curb

"....is that we'll dump something on them & say that they shot first."

landlord & tenant turn away. the menu guy arrives.

i am left with only the sun to argue with. nothing *is* permanent.

A SUPERINTENDENT'S EYES #74
(edison in context or cooler in the sun)

to be chopped &/or puréed
the things chemicals do inside the body
permanent   couplings   data compiled

a comprehensive stripping away of flesh/gender   gander
   facing yourself   almost faceless every morning or should
we say not withstanding flame

the prime source of the photograph   is the camera
the photograph always in the camera
you screaming phonetics in a blaze
i wonder what your voice is really like
cram me
this is a result of fire
it has to be
what chemicals do outside the body

the phonograph always storing sound

wear yourself like wearing yourself out   inside
& enjoy your own good company when you can   if you can
can you
hear your words any better than i can clearly what is   is
what you've just said can only nod & laugh   i don't know
i didn't get it & neither probably in the dense mystery of
your spirit
   do you   ///   or even care

to be flayed or patently animated
still a son you are become
& always when you look into the mirror
& face the day with all its chemicals
now a part of all that you have left
will it wonder the very air itself now turning after
noon   is cheese a product of the udder
          is butter still well churned

& don't please don't forget to wear your gloves
when touching those things
                                        foreign.

A SUPERINTENDENT'S EYES #75
(nothing to write home about)

home is a good place to be a comfy place to be
is archangel hovering over my head rent free
like omelette is sideshow lands end clue
& lunchtime poem
an opening thru one's alter ego painted wall coverings
me not quite
as i retreat to retrieve the mail

it's the way the day meets the cigarstore indians on every
block the gargoyles the cosmetics & the skirts the coffee bars
cafes the way the colors eat them every calendar year eating
her alive finally that rooftop garden what to feed the guests...
my new sinai...absurd material this icing...the city where a
glass of water costs so much...entry for sumday the 1st of
when...those hi-top sneakers i bought the other day at the
salvation army they walk me places i've never been...
becoming sticky tar under foot construction & renovation
everywhere.....& me still holes in the nozone twilit with the
FOOD CHANNEL running 24 hrs & the rats roaches &
mice on permanent vacation...why can't they put their
garbage in the cans...why do they haveta throw it from such
great heights alla time...?
all those angels have become stunned ghosts inside
their tiny cubicles & god reveals himself to us like double
vision on a radio full of static the astronomical rents these
faded hi-tops dumpsters full of souls liquor stores
vegetable stores name brands east west south north same
mortgaged sun potted plants psychic porkchops organ

grinders organ donors skin cancer unbroken me alone on
the fire escape trying to escape

summation: you know i can still LOVE some things & not
love others

A SUPERINTENDENT'S EYES #76
(eclipse)

the snow on the tv gathers.
the words **"REVOLUTION ENDED"**
bounces around my proletariat
brain.

your mouth is open
the sky overcast.

let's look for the moon
i suggest
there's supposed to be an eclipse
tonight.

o.k.   you say
& your mouth closes
around a smile.

gathering ourselves together
we grab flashlights
& begin our
ascent.

reaching the top
we close the door
behind us.

staring upward

clouds gather
& rush by
as we in earnest
search out the moon.

kiss me   i say   & you do.

A SUPERINTENDENT'S EYES #77
(shifting portraits)

APT. #1 — self-styled ineffectual intellectual poet-type super & his artsy asian wife. frankie calls them FARTISTS.

APT. #2 — gay Columbian male "subletter" cooks every night at 3A.M. one in a long string of gay hispanic men or women. he's cute & has many boyfriends. the one before him was ugly & vicious would always sweep the dirt from his house into the hallway. nice guy. no tips. (update: we no longer get along.) a long way back the manager of the rock group Mountain dwelled there.

APT. #3/4 — many different occupants — used to be 2 apts the smaller of which belonged to the old super...the other had dancers...actors ..a heavyset big woman that i slept with a couple of times & saw my first Herzog film (Stroszek) with… now converted into one apt...landlord's older daughter lived there until she died of brain cancer…the landlord bought out son-in-law renovated it — it went from being occupied by 3 english investment bankers to all manner of post NYU wall street types...no problem except for loud drunken parties at all hours & lots of garbage. none ever tipped. duplex. backyard. huge rent. they're partying right now.

APT. #5 — was occupied by old italian lady Mary who lived there for 50 years, was always wonderful to me & whose family owned the building in the 1st ½ of the mid-20th century & sold it due to the depression before my landlord obtained it.

after she passed her sometimes belligerent hiv positive christmas carol singing bi-sexual grandson who worked for the n.y. times took it over. he was rent controlled but hadn't paid his rent in yrs. made all kinds of demands…smoked tons of reefer. had a great dog named lady. always got his demands met...he & i have gotten into huge screaming fights many times... flooded me a few times once from his 50 gallon fish tank destroying my old laptop & the manuscripts it contained. loved nature. used to take great nature photos. had a green thumb. cooked lousy meatballs. was always "right." stopped tipping though in his last year he gave me some holiday cookies. his name was carmine & he's long since died. after him was a 5 foot 3 well built strange personal trainer & his menagerie of young girls. he actually bought one of my books & a cd from me. then by a quiet corporate woman. now a tall thin handsome eastern european whose waste pipe, at this writing, has overflowed causing water to leak into my kitchen.

APT. #6 — oldest tenant in blding at present — husband a hippy photographer who got cancer & moved to florida… he took pictures of the Stones & people with tattoos & recently sent me a link to his website filled with new york photos i ncluding me & the mrs. we used to play poker together & get high… she's a recovering alcoholic & runs a typing business & does psychoanalysis... she got burned by scalding water after the landlord had the now-deceased alcoholic repair man & failed artist, who was Man Ray's nephew, fix her bathtub faucet. she sued the landlord. won. rent controlled. always bothered me. never tipped.

APT. #7/8 — used to be 2 separate places. #7 rented by a guy on wall st. i really liked. always tipped. set up a bed & breakfast. lots of my friends stayed there. (even yuko's parents. her dad ate his first pastrami sandwich there. i had it delivered from the 2nd ave. deli (now on e. 33rd & 3rd.) landlord hired a detective finally found him out & bought him out...always supported my art — buys all my books & cds...# 8 an artist who was into some guru left & kept subletting. one kid she sublet to had a history of disorders, a fine jazz collection & the bad habit of twisting the heads off birds. another was a hoodlum druggy. landlord hired a detective. found her out. kicked her out. she moved back west reunited with her childhood sweetheart. landlord made both into one apt. rented it to a colleague's son & his 2 friends. all students. they didn't hassle me. no tips from any of the aforementioned...before the artist moved in the place used to be inhabited by an actress who helped finance scorcese's "mean streets" & played the epileptic. the super before me used to terrorize her as he did almost everyone else. he also claimed that he fucked her a couple of times. later after moving, she financed "after hours." now the place is occupied by a tiny barking designer dog & its two night owl party parents.

APT. #9/10 — has been a double apt. as long as i can remember. first there was a mad scientist living there who wired the whole place including his front door with an elaborate alarm system & other crazy gadgets. i had wanted to move in when he left some 20 years ago but could not afford the key money. he sold the lease to a pleasant young redhead who lived there for awhile with her boyfriend. they had a kid & sublet the place to a very nice communist heavy metal carpenter who moved in with his girlfriend & their beagle. she loved the dog more than him & eventually left him for a woman taking the dog with her. he had visitation rights & the dog sometimes stayed with him. it eventually died. he developed chronic fatigue syndrome as a result of all this & suffered for about 3 years until he finally met his present wife. she's an eastern european with a grown son who's a d.j. the carpenter & his wife had their own child called romeo. they're all very sweet. the landlord took them to court to try to evict them as illegal subletters & even though they lived there for years they lost. he gave them a year to vacate & said they could live rent free or take 10 grand if they left before the 1st of january. they opted for the year. he was always a good tipper. the 2 before him never tipped. ended up he changed his mind went for the 10 gs instead. after him a young woman caterer moved in with her gay brother. she eventually married a nice quiet guy & they have a wonderful baby daughter. all 4 live in harmony.

APT. #11 — right-wing prejudiced blonde haired blue eyed small towner described earlier in this text...loves guns & good living. is sometimes very demanding other times very pleasant. fancy gardener for a prominent museum & gets the wife & me in free though always has to remind us of that. screenwriter by whim actually had one made into a film. we've had many fights. one physical for which i was arrested. lives now with a black woman. (all this will be explained later) her son, who went to military school & then, iraq, is a fine good soul who has helped me out a few times. he married a lovely girl & has 2 kids. right now #11 & i are getting along fine. tipped once when he needed a big favor. rent stabilized. toilet in hall.

APT #12 — empty for many years then rented out to a quite down-to-earth young lesbian couple. writers. were here quite awhile. never asked me for anything. never tipped. at present i have no idea who the occupants are.

APT. #13 — last was a young mexican-american hustler dressed well had cute hustler girlfriends. owed many months rent. screwed his roommate out of money. both snuck out. never tipped. an Arabic who owned a nearby restaurant lived there for awhile. also snuck out in middle of night owing much rent. 2 lovely looking young women lived there. recently left. they never bothered me nor did they tip. before these this apt. & apt. #14 were both rented by a strange woman who was a folk singer veterinarian who had many ferrets. she knew Roger McGuinn. his wife, Muffin, used to stay with her. she wrote a song called "Living In the Country" that Tom Rush recorded. she, the tenant, had a gruff side. she always wanted a kid so she had one. a boy. sweet. his name is Taylor. she wanted to become a doctor. & she did very late in life. she got breast cancer & died. she used to sublet one of her apts. she never tipped. now occupied by the former tenant of apt.17. refer to that.

APT. #14 — was occupied by 2 brothers who worked for God's Love We Deliver. 1 brother has tattoos from head to toe. this embarrassed him until tattoos became a craze again. musicians i think...started an antique business got very rich…moved out. sublet to their gorgeous "cousin" who had 2 very well groomed ugly chinese dogs...pleasant… no hassle...no tips. when she left i lost track.

APT. #15 — had been a nasty little frenchman who drove his neighbors crazy though he never bothered me. was always at least 5 months behind in his rent. never tipped. finally skipped out. left a nice peacoat behind that i am still wearing. after having the place painted & rewired, a friend of the landlord's daughter moved in. photographer. really nice guy. before the frenchman a mentally ill old lesbian lived there with her on & off normal wonderful warm lover. they were both good writers & gay rights activists way before it was fashionable. they published a newsletter called big apple dyke news. the crazy one was always in & out of the hospital & when not taking her medication would drink heavily & go completely berserk. sometimes she would write weird political graffiti all over the hallways with a huge black magic marker.. i.e. McCarthy slept with Nixon, or things about how the c.i.a. was out to get her because she was the daughter of a corrupt aristocratic Argentinean general (which was true). her place was a wreck & she would shit in the bathtub rather than go to her toilet in the hall. well one day she set the place on fire & they took her away. she was rent controlled. because she was a ward of the state the landlord could not evict her...so after a long court battle he finally bought her out. as can be imagined she never tipped. but when she left she left behind many books including a beat up copy of Pull My Daisy on top of her refrigerator that i now own & have had signed by almost every participant in the film.

APT. #16 — an actor who worked as a draftsman. sometimes asked for super type things. loved jazz. consigned me lots of vinyl when i was selling stuff on the street. has given me a couple of cds on occasion. bought my wife flowers. is mentioned earlier in text. was rent stabilized. recently retired, married an old flame, inherited a family & moved to a little place he bought in new orleans that he'd been going to for the past few years. his apt. under renovation @ this writing.

APT. #17 — she's a single gal in her 40's. been here awhile. beginning of the new wave of tenants with rents over $500. used to work for the big apple circus & after that for broadway productions. always very nice — rarely bothers me. tipped in the form of comps. sometimes is gone for extended periods. always leaves pleasant women in her stead.recently had a major operation to straighten her spine. before she moved in the coolest weirdest old creole lady lived *there. she had the greatest accent. her apt. was painted shocking pink. she had a gate that separated her kitchen from her 2 small backrooms. behind that gate she kept 5 or 6 dogs of various ages & sizes. she fed them in that room. never let them out. she offered me food & stuff. bought things from me. tipped. her name was Miss Emily. she finally died. since this earlier description this apartment was taken over & combined with another top floor apartment to create with the roof a castle for the landlord's daughter. the single gal's still single & now lives in apt.13.*

APT. #18 — well that was andrew, the guy who wrote that great letter in the beginning of all this. he paid at the time the highest rent. the landlord had a rooftop patio built during renovations by frankie & that now dead alcoholic who was Man Ray's nephew so as to entice someone like andrew to move in & pay top dollar. the patio was a wreck & a ripoff. carmine used to walk right over the ledge to water his plants which were on a neighboring roof so andrew's rooftop privacy was almost nil even with a separate locked door. there was direct access thru the apt. from a spiral staircase also built at that time. the roof steps were about 10 feet from andrew's door. he still works for conde nast & is an editor at aperture magazine — is a wonderful guy & was a great tipper. when the first edition of this book came out he bought ten copies. he moved from here to real luxury in tribeca with his equally fabulous Australian girlfriend. i've seen them twice in the past 5 years. he came by the apartment recently & bought most of my books & cds. before he moved in, joey, carmine's cousin had lived there with his mother for over 50 years. he was a long shore man. smoked big cigars. was rent controlled. after his mom died he eventually moved to new jersey to live with his girlfriend. he was already 60 or so by this time. he left the house a total wreck & left in it a bunch of feral cats that he would come back to feed every couple of weeks. the landlord after constantly pressing me for info which i did not give him hired a detective to trace joey. he did. joey was found out & willingly gave up his lease. he died soon after & the task of cleaning out his place & disposing of the cats fell to me. a poet friend who by coincidence was also called joe & who, like me, was an ex-junkie, had a crazy wife that he had met through rehab. she happened to be in animal rescue so we saved the cats from death though they were so messed up they both died within a month of their rescue. joey was old school. warm & like andrew a good tipper. toilet in hall until andrew moved in. now this too is part of the landlord's daughter's penthouse.

APT. #19 — various tenants. sci-fi book collector phd turned fruit deliverer who I knew since childhood and whom I worked for for a while delivering fruit. politcal activist who put in new plumbing illegally & flooded the people downstairs. novelist cook. fat academician. famous yugoslavian poet. neo-nazi german who kept threatening to kill his neighbor & who stole my mail & left me death notes. suicidal advertising executive, etc. at present i have no idea who lives there. had tub in kitchen & toilet in hall. none to my knowledge ever tipped. now has been combined into one unit with apt. 20.

APT. #20 — various. rock band. banker. small time hood. empty for a long time. then forgettable tenant who sublet to an ex-drug addict ex-jazz drummer lesbian with her old very sick dog named joe (yet another joe) that she carried up & down the stairs & who peed all over the place. i, of course, was left to clean up after it. when the landlord found out she was subletting he offered her a lease. she was the last to get in before the rents skyrocketed. she always caused problems. always calling housing inspectors. landlord really regretted being so nice to her. actually tipped once. after she left it remained vacant & now has been combined with apt.19. aside: once the landlord's dead daughter's dog shit in the front hall. she wouldn't clean it up so i rubbed the shit all over her door.

Storefront East & Storefront West — i first visited the blding in the late 60's when the super before me had already lived here & was then one of my best friends. storefront east was an african boutique & s.f. west an antique store. when i moved in, they had been taken over by another of the super's really good friends & made into one space, half for living & half for the first art gallery in soho called fear of art. this was the very early 70's & soho was not really soho but was still the south village. he, the proprietor, was an ex co-founder of daytop village, the first male in vassar, a singer-songwriter, complete with band, poet, novelist, porno writer & one of the earliest A.I.D.S. casualties. he's been dead quite some time now. we looked a bit alike so i once lent him my medicaid card so he could get a hernia operation. (i have since had 3 hernia operations myself & one popped recently.)

after he passed away the place became an italian grocery. the people really came from italy. before opening it the little guy who owned it used to sit in the back of the store with a jeweler's glass on all the time looking at who knows what though i always had my suspicions. they made the best sandwiches & hot lunches around & were very anti-semetic & every other race though he had a tall thin sickly alcoholic irish american friend sleeping & working in the store. "you're not bad for a jew" he'd tell me. he finally disappeared one day. the guy who owned the place didn't want to renegotiate his lease & decided to open up a fancy restaurant across the street.

he also bought the blding where he opened it. this put him in debt. so the second Rocco & His Brothers closed quickly & he lost the blding as well. he reopened another place under an assumed name on carmine st. this one went bust even faster & he disappeared for a long time. i finally found out that he went back to italy where he died of cancer. his wife still lives in the blding next door to me. his kids all moved. i used to take them to mets games with coupons i saved up from the back of milk cartons. i sure miss those sandwiches.

the place then became a locksmith & hardware store. that guy was a psycho, handsome, cokehead & brute. he went out with a lady cop. took over apt. 2 for a while as crash pad & office. in fact that's where i got the indoor outdoor carpet in my living room. he & i were always feuding. he constantly threatened to have me killed & have my body dumped in the woods in canada. he did this to other tenants too. unfortunately he was at this time the landlord's right-hand man. he did any work in the blding that needed to be done or at least contracted the work out. my toilet a case in point. he also took over ¾'s of the basement for his own needs. store supplies, etc. after having many problems & arrests he abandoned the store though the landlord would use his services on occasion. now he's long gone. his name was steve. ironic. thankfully, i think, my body is still here & not in the woods.

after him the store was made into 2 stores again with huge rent hikes. the first 2 were clothing designers, one israeli the other chinese. the chinese woman (s.f. west) was gorgeous. she took over the front ½ of the basement & used it as a sweat shop. it kept getting flooded. she finally got pissed & left. it is now the shoe store whose loud music i hear at this very moment thru the floor. it is owned by israelis. they constantly mingle their garbage with mine. they never tipped though i did them lots of favors. our relationship went from shaky to stable after many close calls. s.f. east's a designer. we get along relatively well. when i say relatively i mean not at all actually. when she heard about the first edition of this book she wanted to buy a copy. i gave her a copy & she said she'd pay me later. instead she returned it the next day said thanks but she read it & felt there was no need to buy it. since then i barely speak to her. she's had many problems that for the most part have been worked out with the landlord with minimal involvement on my part. there were, however, several incidents in which her husband & i got into verbal arguments: see sup eyes #64 part 2 for an extreme example.

many of the above apts. were warehoused for months, sometimes years at a time. yuko used one as a studio for awhile. there were others that i let friends & acquaintances stay in for varying periods of time rent free without the landlord's knowledge. twice i took money from people. what amounted to trifling sums. once the landlord caught a dear friend of mine in one & threw him out. some of these folks bought me presents. like bill the distant relative of the kennedys who lived in one for 4 months. a real slob. he bought me a portable tape recorder with speakers. a cd player & a cd of the philip glass soundtrack to mishima. a film i really enjoyed. the recorder & cd player have both been malfunctioning for quite some time. during this period the landlord tried to co-op the blding. the tenants took him to court & won.

A SUPERINTENDENT'S EYES #78
(the art of craftsmanship)

after many a freezing winter, i finally received new windows. partly for cosmetic reasons. partly as pay since i draw no salary & other than free rent & a charge at a local hardware store receive no benefits of any kind i figured i deserved them. so i asked the landlord & since he was putting them in a couple of newly renovated apts. he agreed.

john, the usually more than efficient window man, was called in. he measured me & one newly vacated apt. we chatted. he said he'd get me screens which were not an option in the other apartments & he left returning after 2 weeks, early on a saturday morning to install them. yuko truly admired his craftsman's spirit as did i.

all the windows were done with the usual elegance & snap. but this one window in the bedroom was unusually small & what normally took him about 1/2 an hr. took, in this particular case, 3...chopping...framing...sawing...putting in new wood...leaving gaping holes in the wall & window ledge. holes left for me, the no talent handyman, to fill before the frost set in.

as he struggled, (the first time i've ever seen him do so), john said to me & his son, john jr., who helped him out on every job, "this is the hardest window i've ever done in my life." & we believed him.

my unswerving faith in him diminished. & with it more of my faith in the working class.

& my desire to be a true bourgeois heightened
along with my desire to be homeless

& my desire to be my neighbor's dog
& the dead water bug near the fuse boxes
& one of those 4 pigeons
swaying like leaves on the leafless tree
in the middle of winter
that i watched this morning
thru the small new window
in my bedroom.

A SUPERINTENDENT'S EYES #79
(here i am)

i've lived here for the past 35 yrs & have been super about 1/3 that time. i took the job over from my old dear friend when he flipped out. i did it as a favor to help him as i had done other times in the past. only this time he left the blding for good & i got stuck with the job which i've done rather poorly. he would sometimes, in paranoid frenzies contact me accusing me of stealing his job & causing him to lose his apt. he even went so far as to threaten to kill me. in actuality i tried to protect him though he was extremely close to the landlord & i wasn't. (i once even told the landlord that his type was the reason why nazis killed jews. he later interpreted it as me having called him a nazi.) well my friend finally got bought out after i covered for him for several months. he & i truly loved each other. in fact he got me this apt. after i got out of rehab. i saw him recently. he has finally fulfilled one of his dreams & started a rock band. he sometimes opens for pete seeger. one of the songs he wrote & sings is about me, this building & how he wants to kill me. i think it's called "spring street." after a recent concert he gave in kenny's castaways in our old greenwich village stomping grounds, he told me how brave he thought i was for having sat through that song. a double exorcism perhaps.

A SUPERINTENDENT'S EYES #80
(for a fellow superpoet)

dear alan,

congratulations on the success of your new book. just getting a small book published myself called *A Superintendent's Eyes*...my job & life in this dump for the past few centuries. thank the rent god i don't have to collect back rent like you do & at this point in my lackluster career as guardian of the lightbulb less & less tenants bother me... i do very little besides hump the garbage, field some complaints, clean up poop & the remnants left by druggies... i never get tips that's how bad a job i do... & my rent would be so cheap that i don't know why the fuck i still do this any more...not much in the way of job security except for all that free toilet paper i get with my hardware store charge...no pork lo mein for me to scrape off the steps, this building (well rent-wise anyway) has gone too highbrow. but for jc's sake why can't these assholes learn to recycle?

today as i took the garbage out on a slippery wet afternoon what did i find??? an entire garbage bag full of calvin klein, armani, & helmut lang t-shirts...not 3 or 4 but 30 or 40 mostly black (black must be out of fashion) with a coupla pairs of designer pants thrown in.

don't worry when they make your book into a movie you'll own that little dream house you now service............

the day is so immense the sky upended as it falls thru
these middle-aged bones   like inquisition water
uproots the hot forged flower   a life wasted?

ponder & wander thru the object world feel think
less more love fame women everything most best
seconds happen tragic or not working lessons
so tired of this tired of this damned rain

they leave
they come back
we accept them

i feel like i am getting too old to write poems

old someone called me today
unedited & old

the leaves
they come back
we accept them

awaiting your words

A SUPERINTENDENT'S EYES #81
(old coat)

1.

there's more here than just frayed buttonholes
& bottomless pockets
there's the wind & dirt of a neighborhood
woven into the long-tamed tweed
& the buying & selling of sanity,
a once abundant item that is no longer at stake.

2.

JUST MENTION :

the bath the gene pool
the steel clear air
the pole the petal the pistol
the staircase the long sweeping walks
a nice greeting & the way the wires tangle about
our feet
& i swear i'll sing to you
with my
DOO WOP

tongue.

A SUPERINTENDENT'S EYES #82
(beauty parlor stroke syndrome)

we all have it   done hair
again   (the benign yet shattering silence before a storm)
                    craft
                              shot zone love buck
   the evil fool out mailed   favorite lava lamp gone limp
                         deep velvet red or incandescent blue
     war documentary store bashed & aching ex-static cling
          your address in my phonebook but not in my head
                 now the wind blowing   public
          for instance   sky darkens as its bladder slowly fills
                              k   a   r   a   t   e
                         slowly   r
                                    kens

   the evil fool outmails the note parking on the outside line
sure i know people   but i know people   the way i know people
shy unrestrained   out   sider   funded privately
                                    shattering the silence

          it gets darker as the sky's bladder fills
         i can't get anything done in the building or the house
          i'm thirsty & want ice cream
                                  (thirsty & want ice cream)
                                         sky darkens
  seems to be darkening forever storm takes so long to arrive
        like warm sex on a hot afternoon
                              snappy but just with other dogs

Shampoo   lean back   but don't lean back too much   & **Rinse**

aching the sky so slowly falls   more like the end of something
than a beginning.

A SUPERINTENDENT'S EYES #83
(another carol)

1st ¼ of the evening we spoke of *close encounters*
she went & helped the other "intellectuals" in the kitchen
i was alone with Marion, Pierre, Pywackit, Sharon & the Camera.

2nd ¼ of the evening she said "i never saw anyone eat like you"
i laughed nervously, cautioned that i was only pretending to eat,
that crowds made me jittery, that i could never fill up at a
strange table.
everyone chuckled.

3rd ¼ of the evening i said "what are you staring at?"
she said "i never saw anyone eat as much as you do."
i said "what?"
she said "i never saw anyone eat the way you do."
i said "i'm not eating — i'm drinking."
she said "where do you put it all?"
i patted my stomach grinned a fat grin & said
"anyway this is only my third glass of apple juice. that's your
fourth glass of wine —
where does it go?" we said almost together
"well the apple juice goes to your/my stomach. the wine
goes to your/my head."
she said "yes. the wine is light. the apple juice is heavy."

4th ¼ of the evening she said "good night. it was a pleasure
to meet you."
"yeh." i said shaking hands & smiling.
"maybe next time we meet i'll eat you under the table."

A SUPERINTENDENT'S EYES #84
(judgement day)

you know what i worry about a lot? now this may seem funny to you oh man maybe even hilarious but i worry real hard about **"JUDGEMENT DAY"**
you know knocking on the pearly gates & all…sure i'm always judging myself
sometimes i think that's all there really is but i certainly do **worry a lot about the** "OLD MAN" up there like maybe he says "you had the heart kid but you just didn't use it." or "you lied too much." or "you had the head but that seemed to get burnt out somewhere along the way." or "you weren't generous enough." or "you certainly had the soul but you spent too much time being petty & sneaky in a really gutless sort of way." & then **"He"** says "you're gonna have to suffer some more kid. like maybe a stint in **Purgatory**. or scrubbin' down the pearly gates or changin' their lock or changin' a washer in the cherubs' locker room or cleanin' up angel shit & dusting off their feathers."
or maybe **"He'll"** let it pass get me some wings that fit just right & let me fly around a bit being the real cute kid that i am. or at least was. or maybe **"He"** won't say anything at all & **"He'll"** just send me straight to "Hell." honestly. i worry about that a lot.

suddenly the can i am lifting slips from my hands & drops on my sandaled sockless right big toe. later that evening in the emergency room i am told it is broken & i wonder if judgement day has arrived sooner than i had imagined.

A SUPERINTENDENT'S EYES #85
(my life as a storage space — shadows/writing)

1. bulk

null & void my fill exo-genesis
the body draped in flag archer
& the cross-legged beauty
pregnancy the experience of summer
  (prematurely)
rolls of undeveloped film swallowing power
degrees — unrelenting miles of cable
the missed connection software hardware
blankets & plastic bags
lps maps handtrucks books
statues chairs linament lifelines
deadlines papers papers papers papers
tests aorta abstract real estate green miles
i don't know how much longer i can keep it all
it's time to learn a trade.

2. lightness

she says that shadows
look much better in winter
than in summer

i say the only time we
are detached from
our shadows
is when we jump.

3. the unbearable bulkiness of light

i was always writing like @ 19 in front of the mirror
on wood roses 3 days on wood roses staring thru the mirror
3 days at a stranger's vanity table swirling pinkblues
heaven & hell @ my shoulders like wings heaven looking
more like hell every instant a stranger's vanity
(heaven/hell)(bluepink) not knowing how to hold on to
what little there was of myself not knowing how to let go
...losses...trying to lessen my losses
learn from my losses hold onto my losses beyond the mirror
toes still playing like music the seeds as they enter my stomach
the poison as it enters my bloodstream like roses
the blood as it leaks from my pen
roses of wood their petals as brittle as paper
their perfume as dull as my (t)horns.

A SUPERINTENDENT'S EYES #86
(time left out)

1.

mt. watermelon. plum. cherry. gum. the plums are not so good this yr. the chinese apples smile. marsh rds. beside marsh fields become marshland. spit seed. the rats chirp in the small side yard. it's 2 a.m. hot. maybe they are arguing over a morsel. or collaborating on a cantata. rain has begun to fall. a slow interrupted rain. the plums are very chewy this yr. not at all sweet. there are highways thru the mts. panels of still lives pits like mts. that dissolve as only mts. dissolve mts. are highways thru the rain. the voices of rats dissolve within the pit of night. i swallow pits & am born again.

2.

i'll need to go out soon & clean up.
i am good at garbage & words.

A SUPERINTENDENT'S EYES #87
(the fear of death for real — HEP C 1–7)

HEP C 1 — idolatry

i drink but cannot get drunk
i am from another world but still
do not know it
the bench i sit on squeaks
i am infected by
my "sins" & the "sins" of others
i ask only to be cleansed
but it is too late
i would like to say that i have enjoyed every moment
but in truth
would much prefer
to do it all over
i am infected by my past
i should redeem myself
but can never be a pious man
sitting here in temple
makes me cold
my neck
shivers
i feel exposed
i realize that the hypocrites
will always remain in power
hypocrite that i am

the rabbi is a whore

HEP C 2 — trick or treat

i guess it's already written
when i'll die
everyone wears a mask today
the parade is winding
down
the old ranting poet
who's not sure who's who
but who's sure he knows what's what
is an hr late
i've been interrupted so much
while attempting to live
that one more interruption more or   less.....................

HEP C 3 — pleasures

she won't drink from my glass
or taste my mashed potatoes
after all these years
our lives have come to a halt
as we begin to live again

leaving the restaurant   i leave
my glass   behind   my plate
behind   my spoon   my cup
my
napkin   behind   my lips
my behind
belongs to the future
now
as i carry my follies forward

HEP C 4 — for m.c.

contaminated
condemned
i spit on the street
shuffle the cards
this is the one that predicted
the dictator's downfall

the rabbi is a whore
the old poet a whore
the sculptor collaborates
with god

are we all whores? would any of us
collaborate with the nazis
to save our own skin for a day?
i tell matthew
"you've learned a lot
you've seen it all before
you've been around
long enough
when it gets to the point of corruption
i know that you will back away."

HEP C 5 — prospects

"you're always talking about death"
"how long?" i ask
"as long as i know you"
"i once or twice died already" she says

HEP C 6 — the final solution (a false alarm*)

only a trace of history   can be found in the blood
the golden calf   the money lenders
i can talk to you again
i can breathe down your throat
i can seed your vagina
i can make you drink my piss

the plague is behind us   for the moment
an oh so casual moment
but don't get too relaxed
for war is still to
come
i can come where i want to now
go where i please for the time
being
time being what it is.

* i was told a week later that i did not have hep c only a trace of it.

A SUPERINTENDENT'S EYES #88
(summer's end)

a.

at summer's end i pick up 3 smooth stones by the shore
one black — one white — one grey
once no doubt used as currency
natural fabrics — the current is strong today
i try talking to the gull in its own language
or an approximation thereof
i'll trade you these stones
for this ocean & this beach i say but get no response
so after a few frustrating moments i mutter
ok so i'm no st. francis or rockefeller or pilgrim
but at least tell me which one of your friends
stole the blue (potato) chips off my blanket
while me & the mrs were takin a dip?

realizing that all this proves fruitless i ask a passerby if they would
snap a few pictures of us standing beside the body of the
newly drowned man.

b.

later that night there's a big fire around the corner
from where i live
she runs back in to get her hysterical cat
she being quite hysterical herself

here do you want to call your friend he asks her
to tell her her apartment was destroyed?
the man had pink water moccasins on before he drowned
one lay beside him & the other was nowhere to be found
she wanted to get back in to save her software
her hardware & her jewels
do you want to let your friend know that all is gone
though all is not lost
except of course for the drowned man —
after much heavy black smoke the roof finally bursts into flames
& shortly after caves in —
the other pink shoe was eventually located by the shoreline
both building & shoe are by this time
totally waterlogged —

i flew toward the horizon & the gull remained
in possession of its senses.
that afternoon
the sun though somewhat clouded over remained golden
that evening the moon though somewhat clouded over
remained golden
& the 3 smooth stones remain resting until this day
upon my window ledge.

A SUPERINTENDENT'S EYES #89
(quartet for the end of time + 1 — food)

1. at a local café — here comes mingus there goes trane

i suffer from rediculitous — a sound & sore kidney with a
stone the size of a baseball where the old lady punched me
& a way too expensive but huge serve-yourself breakfast
where they call your name when the meal's ready in a
dressed down hick-style atmosphere in the heart of
greenwich village in a café full of "hipsters"
with beards tattoos & lumberjack shirts where ella nina billie
& monk fill the space quietly rising above the clatter &
chatter — but man these white kids sure can cook —
the maple syrup's hot & the bread's the softest i've ever had
                                        then the bad music begins

2. goat cheese & leeks (brunch) — for g.c.

i sit across from myself   empty plate
discuss the names of strangers
even those in my blood with a friend
discuss friend with myself
take out ad on invisible sheet of a once blooming tree
have parts of my life stolen from me by myself
by friends by strangers that i do not even get to see
i am up to nothing i practice at being up to nothing
the sun is up in the middle of this
i pay taxes to the perceived of which i am

the same as myself   the empty plate removed
the glass   drained the lemon squeezed beyond its content —

your ashes will go to rome
my flesh will end up in a common grave if i do not act soon
i must get up & pay the check people are waiting
for this table.

3. at a not so local jazz club

in the dark @ the jazz club 2 guys in suits eat something
exotic right down to the bone they suck out the marrow &
wash it down with firewater you can see the bare white
calcium shimmer in candlelight — the flame itself seems like
water sweating in the glass
"more people imagine the end of the world than the end of
capitalism" — her words ringing in my head — the glass
sweating — me sweating as dark arms in dark flannel with
white shirts & striped ties whiskey themselves up — they eat
animals that they barely tolerate — whiskey & bear — their
animal intolerance of beasts — what difference does it make
how we eat our ribs? the difference is the margin between
the civilized & the uncivilized — a fork clicks against a plate
— i am not nor ever will be the standard bearer of good taste
or social etiquette though i consider *my* taste of a high caliber —
the pianist's fingers in the mirror & in real life are the only
standard i can bear right now as he bares it all & i wolf down
his music — it's a slow tune both savage & civilized — as the
set comes to a close i slowly turn my attention away from the
wildly civilized creatures in suits lick my paws with relish &
enter the city of jungles....

4. 14th street green market sequence

at the green market it all looked so good
i decided not to buy a thing
due to the warmth of the market i remove my hat & gloves
buffalo jerky "it's what the indians ate." he tells me

delicate small potato:
purple outside
as well as
inside

red radish:
sun
hurtle me home
ward

buy from a local vendor,
why?   because
the country is right there
on 14th street!

i walk from the green market to my local supermarket
& upon arrival discover that over night it had become
something else. just like this neighborhood going from
sweatshops to art galleries to trendy stores in a blink.
after consuming all these changes with eyes stomach intellect
& heart i decide that i deserve a treat after all the hard work
i've put in picking up trash fighting the elements & dodging
insults & complaints from tenants & landlord alike. i head
for a local bar.

5. scraps

julien,
i am alone in the bar waiting for my meatloaf
like my day & life in general i have been disappointed again
this time it's because they're out of mashed potatoes
they boiled up a new batch & have started to peel them
but the waitress says they won't be ready for an hr
when i arrived home today i gave the halls the once over
then called a dear friend
he said let's have lunch friday
i said fine until he demanded that i meet him in a restaurant
he favors in brooklyn
no way i said you come here i wake up too late
it'll be a hassle going back & forth
& by the time i'd get home my day would be shot
the salad's arrived & i'll have to have fries instead of mashed

(ground beef ground zero daily grind)

anyway he said he always comes to manhattan to see me
so i should go to brooklyn to see him for a change
i said i'd think about it
& call him back
i never suspected that this was an issue with him
i thought he enjoyed coming into manhattan
& i hate that tit for tat social shit
the meatloaf's arrived & tastes very mediocre
& though i never wanted false teeth
i could certainly use some new ones about now
i've been constantly thinking about what **to govern**
meant way back when
it is not this country that is bad but its governing body
the bodies that make up the body doing bad things
for the greater good

i've been thinking about this for a long time
it's been happening like this for centuries
so i gave up voting ages ago
we believe what we choose to believe
what we need to believe
there is a greek chorus inside my head
& the meatloaf's darker than the night outside
& just as flat & uninteresting
language is an abstract thing & in the end there is only
abstraction & the words ***sorry we messed up***
since you are so aware of neglected poets maybe you
will keep my work alive after i'm gone that's if you find
anything worth keeping after all i'm a poet nothing more
nothing less & i know what awaits me 'round the corner for
years i've been waiting & nothing's changed the flag gets
filthier as time goes by & the fabric fades & distance puts
distance between things
but we should never be afraid of our dead
yet if there's nothing to be afraid of then why am i so afraid?
is it because we make war to take our minds off war?
the lady @ the next table
talks about not being a great writer
& that maybe when she's 60
she'll turn out something good
& that that would be gratifying
she's tired of turning out yrs of schlock
though it's the most pleasant way to make a living
she's sad because when she talks to her friends back home
they don't get her
they're smart but can't grasp what she's doing
here in n.y. it's different
she's sometimes sorry that she's not that "other thing"
& that it's kind of o.k. to just be mediocre
& that that doesn't mean you can't change from one

to the other
vanity ambition everything enormous
the bar becomes so high staggering amazing
going back home
nothing
the man with her who apparently is the "other"
speaks softly
what's it all mean?
what we have in common is the mashed potatoes
what little there is to truly say
i sit on the fence so i can see both sides
but i've been sitting on the fence so long
that neither side appeals to me
so i'll rise so that someone can say "he's arisen" or "arose"
i've been pedaling the wrong way down a one way street
but then i found out there were infinite directions
accomplishments how did i get this far? the man says
coming back to that
i'm sure the mashed potatoes are ready
now that i'm done with my meal
i want to join their conversation
tell them that substituting fries doesn't work
i'd like to begin this all over again tomorrow
yesterday or was that......i'll think about today later
after decades of sinister plots a sinister plot has been hatched
right in front of us right out front no lies right there on tv
those parts of our bodies do not even try to hide their blemishes
to conceal their deceit ashes mix with slick & we are fed
new heroes to bury
i'll rub the last piece of bread around the rim of my plate to
soak up the remaining gravy
ask for my check & leave

L — steve

A SUPERINTENDENT'S EYES #90
(theory of poetics & retirement or guilty until proven innocent)

they're building from the top down again as well as from the bottom up or rather the top up & the bottom down — gets more confusing every year —
it's all for the landlord's subterranean office which undergoes floods worse than the one noah had to deal with & for the castle that is forever being made over for his daughter who now occupies most of the top floor as well as the roof...it's like a complex math problem — the equation being how far up is down & vice versa — add into that how much tension one can put on this old wreck of a structure before it ultimately collapses. there is no rhyme or reason for any of this except that the cave dwellers at the top & bottom run this ½ sunken rig & they only care about their **now** & no one else's. the shoe store is still here. so's the boutique. the walls have had a coat of primer on them for almost 5 years waiting for the paint job they will never see. the halls are worse than ever. after the landlord stopped taking out the garbage due to a hip operation he hired a local restaurant worker to do it. sometimes his rather sweet grandson does it. his newest handyman is yet another psycho. there are 4 old tenants left in the building all the rest are strangers though 1 or 2 of these speak to me on occasion. a new café opened across the street to our delight. it was japanese with french stuff. we'd sit in it all day & read, write & entertain friends since our apartment has become so overcrowded & rundown. but alas as suddenly as it opened it was gone due to the huge rent

they paid. after all how much croissants & coffee can one sell to raise $16,000 per month. but good news, just this past month another has replaced it. this time a "real" french bakery that sells overpriced sandwiches & fancy little pastries. when i asked one young cute boy who works there why they don't sell baguettes he said curtly "we're not *that* kind of bakery sir." huh? the guy in apt. 11 still on occasion dresses weird. he got rid of the uptight opera diva ages ago & has been living with a great funny, warm, strong, boisterous copper skinned jamaican gal who buys all my books & cds. he recently got hit by a cab & severely injured his leg but never once complained even with the 5 flights of stairs he has to walk every day.

today he knocked on our door to show us the 3 brightly polished titanium screws removed from his leg just hours ago & promised us he'd get us into the picasso show for free despite the long lines.

a short time before i quit this job we had a big fight while i was taking out the garbage. carmine, the guy from apt. 5 (the one who died of aids) called the cops & reported that there was someone attacking me with a gun. when the cops arrived the fight was over & i was alone humping the trash up from the basement. the cops asked what had happened. i told them a tenant had complained to me about something but it all got worked out. they said they had a report of a gun & asked what apartment the tenant was in. i said it was over there was no gun they insisted i pounded on the banister & screamed THERE WAS NO GUN (i have a very short temper) whereupon they threw me against the door of apartment 3 night-sticked me under the neck bloodied my nose cuffed me & dragged me screaming into their patrol car. as we drove off toward the station i kept yelling about my rights etc. they said if you don't shut up it'll only get worse & your uncooperative big mouth is what got you here

in the first place — it reminded me of another incident that happened around that same time — i was caught shoplifting in tower records made a run for it got caught & had to spend time in jail being shipped from one place to another in the middle of a cold rainy night eventually winding up in a cell with a raving lunatic. about 36 hours after my arrest when brought to a holding pen in the courthouse the home boys asked me what i was in for i told them shoplifting & they asked why did i have a habit to support or somethin' i told them no i only stole for my own enjoyment that that's what i got high from at this point in my life at which i got high fives & pats on the back & praises for being so well ya know so... selfless... after being served the worst ham sandwich of my life & shitting & pissing in a bucket all day i was allowed to make a call i was then hauled up in front of a judge with about ½ a dozen hookers. when it came my turn i barely had time to utter a word when the judge pounded his gavel on the podium & said TIME SERVED.
anyway, this time, just before we got to the station the cops looked at me & one of 'em said you better keep your mouth shut about this or else, pointing to my bloody nose. i nodded & looked straight ahead. when we got to the station they dragged me out of the car uncuffed me & sent me on my way.

the leaves were piling up on the street that day just as they do now

a golden carpet she says — come outside & see the guy from apt. 11 makes his way slowly up

the darkening stairs.

A SUPERINTENDENT'S EYES #91
(friday the 13th — the final chapter)

this is only a bad dream but when i wake up it will be friday the 13th

i am in the basement of my building. everything has been removed but one big bag of garbage. i have long since retired from being super and now occasionally the landlord's grandson, freddie, a rather large being who lives in the penthouse on the roof with his aunt, the landlord's younger daughter, takes out the garbage. his mother who used to lock him in the closet is long dead. his father still does work in the building renovating newly vacated apartments so the rents can be astronomically raised. the basement glows an eerie clean greenish color, as does the green plastic garbage bag. i approach it to bring it outside along with the other bags that i assume freddie has hauled out earlier. the season is unclear though it feels like summer. the bag is open and filled to the brim & i struggle with its neck to tie it up. try as i might it seems almost hopeless. finally i pull the ends tight & thin & manage to get it knotted. i start to drag it toward the stairs when i feel an ominous presence looming behind me. i turn & see freddie, eyes lit up, with a maniacal grin on his face. he stretches his left arm toward me in a frankensteinian gesture. i start to lug the bag harder breaking into a sweat. i turn to look at freddie again. he suddenly rubs his right thumb against his forefinger starts a small blaze & proceeds to ignite his hair laughing now under his breath while still advancing. suddenly, in orangy cotton-candy-clown-like tufts, his hair begins to fall away from the sides of his head, revealing a shiny perfectly rounded scalp. i reach the stairs, huffing & climbing, freddie close behind. i start quietly yelling for my wife "yuko...yuko... yuko..." as i round the top of the stairs & pull toward the entrance, with freddie in hot but slow pursuit. as i reach the main entrance, numb & chill with horror, i fling open the door with one hand, holding the bag in the other. my apartment is in the front & at that instant yuko opens our door & asks "what's the matter?" freddie's hand is just about to grab me or the bag when... *i pull the pillow closer to my chest...*

we are in the midst of an oppressive heat wave
i'm reading dostoyevsky's **THE DOUBLE**
i especially love that little spot behind her ear that will never get tanned

this is Friday the 13th but when i wake up it will be tomorrow
& tomorrow will always be Friday the 13th

A SUPERINTENDENT'S EYES #92
(addendum[b] — night viewing)

1.

people just too weird   they dance for nothing
when ritual become nothing — a mark on the floor
that can be approached but not gone beyond
they eat for nothing & love for nothing & sing for nothing
are good for ...wednesday...let's get together wednesday
          "i can't i have to bury my mother's ashes"
well does that take all day?   for people are good for ashes

2.

birds dance
people weird try to be things for nothing
costumed in health —
me take my rotting body to its end
don't try don't be use the limited language given me
people fly wings afire — burn for nothing
poor kids @ the end of their dance — for nothing
"to shit" he says
thin line on a thinner wall > people do things for nothing
to be something   "a safe house"
whose holocaust is this anyway? i will stink by my end anyhow
by way
suicideling along in this fantasy of why i think i do things
a spot on the floor for the dancer to step within

collide-scopic shadows   stepped within
people weird   they sing for nothing

3.

the star is over   has crossed the belly
has laid hands on & left…directions
but the routes are abandoned —
people build roads for nothing

4.

night viewing the cherry blossoms
illumined by their own pink light
for nothing.